The Legacy of
Raymond Unwin:
A Human Pattern
for Planning

The MIT Press

Massachusetts Institute of Technology,
Cambridge, Massachusetts, and London, England

The Legacy of Raymond Unwin:
A Human Pattern for Planning

edited and with an introduction by Walter L. Creese

Preface

THE assembling of this material probably began the day I visited Mrs. Edward Unwin, the daughter-in-law of Raymond Unwin, in the family home, "Wyldes," at the edge of Hampstead Garden Suburb. She still had some of his papers which I was permitted to deposit in the library of the Royal Institute of British Architects (RIBA). It is from these that the hitherto unpublished quotations of earlier authors, his models, and the excerpts from the "The Dawn of a Happier Day" (1886) and "Gladdening v. Shortening the Hours of Labour" (1897) come. Mr. James C. Palmes of the RIBA library and the officers of the Institute helped and encouraged this initial venture.

Mrs. Curtice Hitchcock, Unwin's daughter, made his portraits available and checked the dates. She also talked to me enough so that Sir Raymond became a substantial person in my mind. Mrs. Barry Parker assisted, as often before, by lending the picture of the Parker and Unwin families. It was a fortunate day when first Mr. Lewis Mumford and then Professor Nikolaus Pevsner directed me to her house at Letchworth, for she had kept her husband's records meticulously, and she shared with me many personal recollections of the partnership of Parker and Unwin.

The quotations and illustrations from the articles and books are reproduced by permission of the Parker and Unwin families and the various organizations and companies which originally published them, as duly noted at the head of each section and in the captions. Exceptions are the actual slide prints from Unwin's Columbia University Lectures which were assembled (as many as could be found) and generously lent by Professor Ronald W. G. Bryan of the Institut d'Urbanisme of the University of Montreal. Professor George Collins, Adolf Placzek, Avery Librarian at Columbia, and Mr. Carl Feiss helped with the Columbia material.

The painting by Seurat comes from the National Gallery in London and the Norwich Wallpaper from the Victoria and Albert Museum.

Others have not only assisted with typing and checking but also have suffered from the tedium of this kind of effort to make another's lifetime of thought evident and communicable. Foremost among them were my wife, Eleanor, my son, Guy, and Mrs. Edith Diehnel, Mr. Larry Arnold, and Mrs. Frances Newsom of the University of Oregon.

Without research grants from the Fulbright board and the Rehmann Fellowship Committee of the American Institute of Architects, the book could not have occurred.

Walter L. Creese
Eugene, Oregon, February, 1966

Contents

Illustrations

Introduction

xi

The Legacy of
Raymond Unwin:
A Human Pattern
for Planning

Chronology of
Sir Raymond Unwin
(1863-1940)

1863
Born November 2 at Whiston, near Rotherham in Yorkshire, north-east of Sheffield, England.

c. 1882–1883
Apprentice engineer for Staveley Coal and Iron Company near Chesterfield. Attained some notice for his work on pithead baths and miners' cottages in the early 1890's.

1893
Married Ethel Parker, sister of Barry Parker.

1896
Joined Barry Parker in an architectural partnership at Buxton, Derbyshire, in the northeast. Parker had begun his practice there in 1895.

c. 1899–1901
Living at Chapel-en-le-Frith at the "Lodge by the Beeches."

1901
Began New Earswick near York for the Rowntree Chocolate Trust.

1903
Began Letchworth Garden City after a competition with Halsey Ricardo and W. R. Lethaby. Plan competition sponsored by the Rowntree family.

1903
"Cottages Near a Town," exhibit for the Northern Art Workers' Guild of Manchester.

1905–1914
Worked on Hampstead Garden Suburb near London for Henrietta Barnett and others. Took up residence at the farmstead of "Wyldes" there, which remained his home.

1909
First Housing and Town Planning Act passed under guidance of John Burns. Published *Town Planning in Practice* in partial response to it, although the book had been in preparation for some years.

1910
Organized International Town Planning Exhibition and Conference promoted by the Royal Institute of British Architects.

1911–1914
First lecturer in Town Planning at Birmingham University as a result of a grant from the Cadbury family.

1913
One of the founders under leadership of Thomas Adams of Town Planning Institute.

1914
Partnership with Parker dissolved. Unwin became Chief Town Planning Inspector to the Local Government Board at the invitation of Sir Herbert Samuel. Parker went to Oporto, Portugal, then to Brazil to work on projects.

1915
One of the founders of the League of Nations Society.

1915–1916
President of the Town Planning Institute.

1916–1918
Director of Housing, Ministry of Munitions. Responsible for Gretna, Mancol Village, Queensferry, and other wartime housing.

1918
Returned to the Ministry of Health as Chief Architect and ultimately Chief Technical Officer for Building and Town Planning. Served on the Tudor Walters Committee.

1922
Visit to America at invitation of the Russell Sage Foundation to consult on the New York Regional Plan to be directed by Thomas Adams. Was probably first in the United States in 1911 or 1912.

1925
Returned again to New York City to attend the meeting of the International Town, City and Regional Planning and Garden Cities' Congress. Also addressed the national meeting of the American Institute of Architects in New York City.

1927
Wythenshawe Satellite City begun for Manchester by his former partner.

1928–1931
President of the International Federation for Housing and Town Planning, following death of Sir Ebenezer Howard. Retired from Ministry of Health in 1928.

1929–1933
Chief Technical Adviser to the Greater London Regional Planning Committee. Affected Greater London Plans of 1943–1945.

1931–1933
President of the Royal Institute of British Architects.

1932
Knighted.

1932–1935
First President of the Building Industries National Council.

1933–1934
Chairman of the British Building Research Board.

1934
In August came to the United States at the invitation of the National Association of Housing Officials to report on low cost housing after a six-week tour of the country. Companions were Ernest Kahn, economist, banker, and former manager of public housing projects at Frankfurt, Germany, and Miss Alice M. Samuel, manager of the housing estates of the Bebington Urban District Council. They were accompanied by Henry Wright and Ernest J. Bohn and stopped in New York, Washington, Boston, Cleveland, Detroit, Chicago, Milwaukee, St. Louis, New Orleans, Atlanta, Knoxville, Cincinnati, Pittsburgh, and Philadelphia. Reported in October 1934 in Baltimore to the N.A.H.O. in time to have an influence on major New Deal legislation of 1935, such as that for the Resettlement Administration and slum clearance and greenbelt towns. The major part of the report was prepared by him.

1935
LL.D. from Manchester University.

1936–1940
To Columbia University in the fall of 1936 to be Visiting Professor in the Planning and Housing Division, following the death of Henry Wright. Also lectured at Cornell and Massachusetts Institute of Technology.

1937
In April received the Gold Medal of the Royal Institute of British Architects.

1937

In June was awarded an honorary doctorate by Harvard University. Other degrees were from Prague (D.Tech.), Toronto (D.Arch.), Trondheim (D.Tech.).

1938

Received the Howard Memorial Medal of the Garden Cities and Town Planning Association.

1939

Appointed Chief British Delegate to the International Congress of Architects in Washington by Neville Chamberlain. Meeting was canceled because of war conditions although Unwin arrived in Washington.

1940

Died in Old Lyme, Connecticut, at the summer home of his daughter, Mrs. Curtice Hitchcock, on June 28th, age seventy-six.

Introduction

THE IDEALS
AND ASSUMPTIONS OF
SIR RAYMOND UNWIN

Walter L. Creese

A COMPLETE list of the speaking engagements and minor writings of Sir Raymond Unwin would hardly be possible. He addressed too many realtors, chambers of commerce, men and women estate managers, social and health service workers, sanitary engineers and summer school students. He submitted too many articles and letters to obscure magazines and now defunct newspapers.

A great deal of the writing was by necessity current and topical. He was a public official from 1914 on, and planning as he conceived it had to be invented as he went. It was also urgent to foster earlier recognition and demonstrate higher impact to justify his system to others. He was an unabashed social critic and activist, and this caused a lot of his writing, particularly from 1885 to 1905, to have a polemic and journalistic flavor. Often it makes better listening than reading.

Several of the problems with which he dealt no longer exist. The railroad station is no longer the focal point for the traffic of most cities and few people still wish to find it. The slum in the United States and Europe, at least, is no longer so physically confining or psychologically threatening. The priorities of the tram or streetcar, the bicycle, the horse, the chimney sweep, the dust and coal men, and the pedestrian have largely disappeared. The working class has risen to the middle. Relations between city and national governments, which were critical to Unwin's method of getting things done, altered noticeably after both World War I and II.

To capture the full course of Unwin's thought without becoming caught in the swirl of by now irrelevant topicalities, it appeared legitimate to reproduce only a selection of his writings, with the important transition points or career markers identified by significant

6

chapters and outstanding articles. The sequence or progression to be gained from this may have a special inference for all planning, insofar as planning is often by necessity preoccupied with the momentary, the immediate and the pressing (as with traffic, housing and utilities), and by the same token frequently carries its intended or accidental momentum on into the next generation and the next. The novelty of planning is that by its very nature it is neither short nor long term, but both. Planners do not starve in garrets, but neither do their dreams come true. They are the unacknowledged captive artists of the modern age. So it is the condition of Unwin's servitude which chiefly absorbs us here, as he becomes increasingly free to propose alternatives but never completely emancipated from actual budgets and circumstance.

Unwin and his partner, Barry Parker (1867–1947), were at times more exceptional to the rule, since they witnessed their dream communities of Earswick, Letchworth, Hampstead, and Wythenshawe and elsewhere rise into being amidst praise and patronage. In this respect they were the most fortunate and typically British architectural amateurs since John Nash or Joseph Paxton.

The inspiration evinced by the writing can go far in explaining the execution of these unusual settlements. But more than that, it helps to outline the permanent character of Unwin after the dust of ancient battles has settled, and that is the real justification for reviving his words today and for trying to reformulate a whole picture of his personality. Anyone who sets out to locate the prominent planners who publicly acknowledge their debt to Unwin—in the United States, John Nolen, Clarence Stein, Henry Wright, Lewis Mumford, and Carl Feiss (who was his assistant at Columbia University, beginning in 1936); from Denmark, Jens Jensen and much later Steen Eiler Rasmussen, who so eloquently described the planning of Unwin in his extraordinary book proclaiming London as a unique city; from Germany, Ernst May, the early and distinguished planner of Frankfurt; and any number of other individuals from Britain, Canada, Sweden, and Holland—will soon be convinced that it is not the specific techniques or actual communities these men appreciated so much as his personal warmth and magnetism. When others flashed and rumbled, he appeared to emanate a quiet glow.

7

The steadiness and resolution of Unwin's character might make him appear in retrospect a little dull, especially to the young and to those historians or critics directly attuned to the political, military, or economic crises of any given decade through which he passed. Yet surprise and excitement are to be found in the very realization that Unwin did not allow himself to become distracted by those immediate and distressing alarms, except by the way in which they might register what he considered the greater social issues. This contrast to other planners is more apparent if he be compared with a contemporary non-planner like George Bernard Shaw (1856–1950). Their do and dare was similar, even though their temperaments and achievements were quite different. Both carried on far-flung public campaigns for numerous causes. Shaw had been attracted by Henry George, speaking on his single tax theory for land in the mid-1880's, just when Unwin gained his first determination about land from Edward Carpenter, much of it derived from Walt Whitman. Among chronically reserved Englishmen they stood out with their knack for visionary elaboration, as their remarks at the Bournville garden city conference of 1901 exemplify. Unwin's interpretation of the current scene might never be so agile or witty as Shaw's, but he also occasionally resorted to oversimplification and paradox. His town plans were further like Shaw's dramas in that the byplay often grew so vivid and entrancing that later audiences came to forget what the main lesson was supposed to be and gave themselves up completely to the entertainment.

Shaw, like Unwin, was a youthful friend of William Morris and admired him enough to publish a little book about that association. He wrote pamphlets for the Fabians, as did Unwin. He also viewed the impending ascent of the working class to the middle class with one eyebrow cocked. He courted socialism and Christianity as potent communal forces but wanted to apply them in unorthodox and individualistic ways. Unwin declared that his commitment to a more organized, Christian, and cooperative society was mainly for guaranteeing and protecting individualism! Individual gifts were sorely needed because society was becoming increasingly large and complicated, and the development as soon as possible of the reliable and self-motivated person was the only sure process for introducing a many-leveled responsibility adequate to the well-being of the whole

8

society. The house or cottage was to be restored as a type to reinvigorate the family, which had been so badly disrupted by the factory systems of the industrial revolution. Each child should thus be prepared by the familial regrouping to take his or her constructive place in society. Art and individualism were to be oddly intertwined or switched from track to track in a manner similar to individualism and communality. Among his personal notes (in characteristic green ink and under a heading of "1884 or 5") appears the following to illuminate the basic assumption:

Either all genuine liberty of life and action will be lost to the individual through enslavement to the impulses of mass control; *or* planning on cooperative lines must be adapted to secure that a free space and sphere may be allotted and preserved for the individual within which he may be free to exercise his liberty and initiative for the *good of all*.

That is planning *design in place* of haphazard!

It will tax man's designing powers to keep pace with the growing needs created by the widespread interlacing of *life interests*.

This is Art!

It is as if he were trying in his youthful and impulsive way to stockpile emotional and psychic capital for the society, which was about to be overwhelmed by external change, brought on by too rapid capital investment and physical accumulation. An impression he was anxious to avoid was that group action implied conformity, but it did involve apparent contradiction, since it meant that individualism was to be reoriented within a lattice of proportional physical planning and true art was the vinicultural interlacing for this frame, to tie people safely in by a less binding and chafing fibre than factory hours and urban ways.

Bernard Shaw knew Ebenezer Howard and had invested modestly in his shorthand typewriter and heavily in his garden city scheme. Barry Parker appears to have added to Shaw's house at Ayot St. Lawrence, near Welwyn Garden City. So the similarities in methods and attitudes were probably more than chronological or fortuitous.

QUOTATIONS

It may have been the necessity to prepare a platform from which to deliver a message which attracted Unwin toward planning and away from architecture, just as Shaw was drawn toward playwriting and away from criticism. To a degree both men were unfulfilled actors and Unwin was a hero worshipper from his earliest days. Like Shaw, too, he had a curiosity about the social uses of the Superman, although it is not clear whether this came to him indirectly from Nietzsche (through Edward Carpenter via Havelock Ellis), from Ralph Waldo Emerson and Thoreau, or Thomas Carlyle. But, unlike Shaw, he approached custom and tradition with deference. He wanted to preserve memories almost as much as he wished to create new possibilities. His individual rebellion was socially important because it was topically profound and became more so over a length of time since his chief activity was double and open ended. The extended phase of planning, which required a good long look ahead, sustained this distinct effort to tie past with future. Shaw, of course, had scoffingly remarked, "He who can, does. He who cannot, teaches." Unwin gave the lie to this oft-quoted formula for ineffectuality by doing both extremely well, although he was also impatient with idle or academic talk about society and environment. He was a teacher and a Briton insofar as he sought to carry the burden of motivation over the gap from generation to generation, perhaps again partly because communities last longer than separate or individual people. The permanent social responsibility delegated to him by Ruskin, Morris, James Hinton, and Edward Carpenter (who called his attention to Walt Whitman and the vision of a swelling and singing democracy), and W. R. Lethaby markedly differentiated him from Shaw, was highly pertinent to the time span of planning, and stayed with him until the end.

"THE DAWN OF A HAPPIER DAY," 1886
"GLADDENING V. SHORTENING THE HOURS OF LABOUR," 1897

Unwin did not really become a practicing architect until he was thirty-three and a planner until almost forty. These original documents confirm what the chronological delay implies, that he was too worried over the condition of man and labor to pay major attention in his early years to formal building activity, the material and

10

frame which could enclose that situation. His attitudes in these two tentative essays are greatly affected by William Morris, to whom he refers as "the great Poet-Craftsman." During these same years he was preaching in the secular Labour Churches of the north, founded by fellow architect John Trevor, on the life and work of William Morris. He also wrote a few articles for Morris' magazine, *Commonweal*.

Unwin believed the eight-hour day would come and the four-hour day suffice if only men could learn to pool their labor, to compete less, and give up the new ambition of making nasty, cheap, and useless goods. But he is more anxious about the surplus leisure the machine will permit than about the material objects it might oversupply.

There is already a dichotomy between what might be the best application of labor and the best use of leisure. The particular type of work and the specific objects made are secondary to his interest in the improvement of the circumstances under which the work would take place. As the two titles suggest, he above all wants gladness and happiness to occur and believes the right path lies in the direction of cooperation rather than competition. His theme is colored by the long-standing bitterness around Manchester about textile and shirt factory conditions and in the Sheffield area over coal and ore mining, both of which he knew at first hand. It carries a tinge of older innocence, too, from the utopian colonies that were founded near Sheffield, especially those of his other heroes, Ruskin and Carpenter, at Totley and Millthorpe. Unwin had been a member of the Labour Brotherhood in the Ancoats slum of Manchester under Charles Rowley and an engineer for the Staveley Coal and Iron Company in Chesterfield, adjoining Sheffield, in the early 1880's. His wish to make work actively joyous so that escape from toil would be less urgent stems partly from Morris. Again he kept a pertinent Morris quotation in his papers, "And that which will be the instrument that it shall work with, and the food that shall nourish it, shall be man's pleasure in his daily labour, the kindest and best gift that the world has ever had." On the back of the manuscript of "Gladdening v. Shortening the Hours of Labour" is a penciled after-comment, "Trade Unions must tackle Quality of work as Guilds did" and below it, "Not yet even touching the constructing," evincing the Morris teamwork principle and, more for the future, Unwin's own habit of hypothesizing practical instruments or agencies for ideas almost as quickly as they came to him.

Since the second essay, "Gladdening v. Shortening the Hours of Labour," was an actual speech to a Sheffield group, it gives an initial opportunity to sample his way with audiences. Simple ideas are expounded, then put together as one. His mind is lucid, but he is slightly handicapped by spelling, punctuation, and a failure to align singulars and plurals. He is also inclined toward awkwardness and pleonasm, as in the phrases, ". . . work that is which is . . ." and ". . . ordinary task work. . . ." It is not clear whether this was the result of haste, a wish to retain an element of folksiness (he enjoyed the word "folk" almost as much as "work"), or the brevity of his early and formal education. Since he was brought up in Oxford, where his father was a tutor, and throughout his life associated with authors and intellectuals, this lack of variety and accuracy in speech or writing could not have been due to having never heard precise English. Carpenter refers to him in his autobiography as a "cultured" young man. Unwin does observe in "Gladdening v. Shortening the Hours of Labour," of 1897, that what is needed for a better society is not a race of students or intellectuals, created by the new leisure (which he spells "liesure" or "lissure"), but a "race of commonsense men and women with all their faculties phisical [sic] artistic and mental well developed. The best education is not to be got from books alone. Nothing so much educates as life and work." Experience, hard knocks, his own and others, always were grist to his thought and sympathy, although his command of language and persuasion improved as he went along. And he never got over his partiality for "commonsense."

PARKER AND UNWIN, *THE ART OF BUILDING A HOME,* 1901

With this first book the cogitation of Parker and Unwin, who had begun their architectural partnership at Buxton in 1896, starts to focus on a specific discipline. In the chapter entitled "Co-operation in Building" the image of the self-contained English village was re-invoked. The essential idea becomes plain in the sentence, "This relationship reveals itself in the feeling of order which the view induces." The whole program depended on the melding of social and visual elements into a coherent synthesis. But there was always a village before, and a village *after,* the industrial revolution for Parker and Unwin.

In a similar fashion in "Building and Natural Beauty" the theory was advanced that modern man was trying too hard to overtop or defy nature and that this was becoming toxic in a cumulative manner, like a poison building slowly up in a large system. Earlier centuries had known how to relate buildings in a landscape as well as to integrate human life in the village. Unwin hoped that a formulating, visualizing, shaping, or grasping ability had become misplaced rather than entirely lost. His contemporaries on the Continent were intrigued by the possibility that this intuitive blending resulted from some sweet urban secret or internal metaphysic dimension of the Middle Ages which they would soon recover.

This rather breathless anticipation extends from the Viennese Camillo Sitte to the Finnish-American Eliel Saarinen. Unwin too was subject to the fascination, but his "commonsense" overcame any reticence in stating why the pretechnological community appeared so fitting to the life it supported. He explained that the harmony in British villages, at least, was the result of a common, careful, everyday attention to details, such as a compatability of materials, the settling into the undulating and protective contour of the hills, and the time-ripened sagging and natural weathering of walls and roofs and, above all, the communal acceptance of the discipline of a physical order which represented a social and psychological self-assurance underneath. Leisure and skills in the past had dealt with the direct and actual instead of the conspicuously romantic or artificial in buildings and communal life. And soon there would be more leisure and skill.

Within *The Art of Building a Home* the stylistic factors are a direct outcome of principles so far stated. The introduction declares that "The essence and life of design lies in finding that form for anything which will, with the maximum of convenience and beauty, fit it for the particular functions it has to perform, and adapt it to the special circumstances in which it must be placed." The concept of form following function was one of the most persistent within the active architectural theory of the last hundred and fifty years.

However, Parker and Unwin wished to employ it widely to involve a whole community or region and more exactly to suit a particular location. They would not be seeking to explore it for universal structural systems or the appropriateness of the new materials of which these ought to be made, as later Continental architects were to do, although Unwin recognized this fairly early in the century as one legitimate goal for modern architecture.

The greatest functional opportunity, so far as Parker and Unwin were concerned, was to be found in the garden city yet to come. But in another attitude expressed in this first book they were thoroughly in concert with most other architectural leaders. The chapter "Art and Simplicity" makes it apparent that the ingredients of purity and frugality were of primary significance for them in a creative, as distinguished from a retrospective, way. A very similar view was held by the men around them in the later British domestic school— C. F. A. Voysey, M. H. Baillie Scott, Ernest Gimson, C. R. Ashbee, George Walton, C. M. Crickmer from Letchworth, and even Edgar Wood and Edwin Lutyens in some of their phases. This attitude was also to have important consequences on the Continent after 1900, particularly at Darmstadt in Germany, through Baillie Scott, who decorated the palace there in 1898. Peter Behrens built a house in Darmstadt in 1901 and Joseph Olbrich another in 1905 that had several features in common with the English houses. These two architects, like their English counterparts, evidenced a great interest in the crafts to furnish their houses. At the moment the house was *the* internationalist building type. The Grand Duke of Hesse-Darmstadt had invited Olbrich up from Vienna in 1899 to begin an artistic colony, a center for modern art. This linked Darmstadt with another of the urban beautifying movements of the 1890's, which found a notable expression in Vienna in the municipal railroad stations of 1894 and 1897 by Otto Wagner. They too featured clean, calm, flat surfaces and materials in an exposed state. The influence was also being reinforced directly from England by Hermann Muthesius, who

14

was attaché at the German embassy in London from 1896 to 1903 and who published a book, *Das englische Haus* in three volumes in 1904 and 1905 (Wasmuth), which had a considerable effect on Germany. Muthesius was also interested in the crafts, mass housing, and standardization. He was a founder of the Deutsche Werkbund. Many of these trends culminated for Europe in the Bauhaus at Dessau of 1925–26, founded by Walter Gropius. Gropius had been a pupil of Peter Behrens.

An early but undated memorandum on housing for Letchworth Garden City (presumably by Unwin) shows this cleansing or purifying rite already operative in both architecture and planning, but not for the sake of an improved technology, cheapness, or standardization. It is asserted rather to strike a proper and difficult balance between a *decent* and a *minimal* cottage in order to assist toward a more wholesome and deep-seated village harmony, a persistent and disturbing problem left in the wake of the technological and urban revolutions which had begun in Britain. "The promoters are convinced that the high standard of beauty which they desire to attain in the Garden City can only result from simple straightforward buildings suitably designed for their respective purposes and honestly built of simple and harmonious materials; they do not seek any artificial attempts at the picturesque, nor do they ask for any useless ornamentation. Buildings of the utmost simplicity will be permitted if suitably designed for their purpose and positions." The primary overlay of the twentieth century is here: frugality superimposed on nineteenth-century functionalism, but it refers to the planner's social and economic expectations more fundamentally than to any technological construct.

COTTAGE PLANS AND COMMON SENSE, 1902

This second book brings the imagery up and out of the utopian promise and ancient village onto the threshold of action, poised for the building of a garden city. But for another moment realization has to be deferred in favor of the development of the theory of the fringe areas and outskirts of cities. The possibility of the control and improvement of outskirts by municipalities had been brought about by the Housing Act of 1900 and by the writing of individuals like W. H. Lever, the soap magnate from Liverpool, who built the model village of Port Sunlight, and T. C. Horsfall of Manchester, who was to publish *The Example of Germany* on this subject in 1904. Parker and Unwin added their bit by publishing a plan and explanation of "Cottages Near a Town" in 1903. It was contained in the Catalogue of the Northern Art Workers' Guild, which was a Manchester offshoot, through Walter Crane, of the Morris Arts and Crafts movement around London and furnishes another indication that these young men regarded planning from the first as a means to a social and artistic end rather than as an independent discipline.

The "Common Sense" included in the title was, of course, the original virtue. Unwin advocates an emphatic action that will bring people to their senses. There was a plethora of irrationality, disproportion, and misdirected impulse in the late nineteenth century in the face of the onrush of urban growth which he simply could not tolerate. The grand ambition of the working class to better its station through styles of living he regarded as a *petite illusion*. He says, "A desire to imitate the middle-class home is at the bottom of the modern tendency to cut the cottage up into a series of minute compartments." It was wasteful and unhealthy and nourished snobbery in reverse. He disliked the general atmosphere of shrewdness and bargaining, the false economy, that the commercial world had generated along with all of its material goods. He wished to stimulate the "gentler and finer instincts of men," he said. The transitory nature of much that was being built in the name of Progress disturbed him, too. He and Parker were willing to limit their practice to the smaller cottage and complete town and omit the intermediate design of large buildings and the professional affluence it might bring them because "only the very best that is known and can be devised today is likely to stand the test of time; and this must be based upon the permanent and essential conditions of life and health, not on passing fashions or conventions established by the speculative builder." A down-to-earth, common-sense, thoroughgoing, functional approach to the housing situation should be bound to yield workable answers. A restudy of tradition would provide a reliable checklist for future urban composition. Cheapness ought to be outlawed. Sanitary and lighting reforms were not going to be enough. As streets became more important, they too should be more carefully and thoughtfully designed, not merely regularized.

This new or simplified attitude on his part resulted most immediately in an attack on the airlessness of back yards and alleys. The southern or sunny orientation was requisitioned for a better outlook for the long-suffering housewife. There was to be a breaking down of the internal divisions of the cottage, as indicated, with the living room and parlor combined and the separate staircase and hall abolished. The through living room and bedroom were introduced to carry on for decades amongst garden city house types, later to be indiscriminately imitated in suburban and county council units. Altogether this signifies the beginning of the abiding sunniness and cheerfulness, tidiness and cleanliness, in smaller British houses which was later regarded by some as wholly insufferable, since the "sunshine" cottages supposedly looked so apple-cheeked and inane. The gesture was toward a more positive mental health, however, and in several senses it was the architectural answer to Unwin's prearchitectural call for a gladder or "happier" day.

In the reopened living room was an inglenook by the fireplace, one of Parker and Unwin's most characteristic internal arrangements, equivalent to their external cul-de-sac street. It was their hope to reconstitute a refuge, a place of retreat when the time of day, the social function, or the age of the residents recommended it, moving toward family or social life or withdrawing from it when privacy was desired to preserve individuality. This rhythm was suggested to Unwin by his reflection upon the model of the great hall of the medieval manor (Figs. 8, 40, 45), also a favorite with William Morris.

But what was happening in a more abstract context was the fashioning of open or generalized space frames or containers, which would later be considerably elaborated. Eventually they came in many shapes and sizes in the Parker and Unwin vocabulary, and were often referred to by Unwin as "crystals"; the central and satellite cities with greenbelts (Fig. 39), the well-organized village, the public square with entrances so placed that they could not destroy the unity of life within the square (Fig. 54), the quadrangle, the close, the cul-de-sac, the inglenook, the bay, the front porch or balcony with seats for the elderly and infirm (Fig. 45).

This self-limiting for the encouragement of personal and meaningful existence was common to all, and profoundly British. Even today the tourist has only to travel from city to city in a British train to discover how useful the newspaper is as a shield for the citizen to protect his individuality amidst the multitude. The train compartment is a larger box for this.

Unwin also indulged in the habit then popular among young thinkers of dredging up broad anthropological conclusions about the contemporary scene through ruminating on primitive man. He probably derived this conceit most directly from the London aural surgeon, James Hinton, although at the time many others were trying their hand. He feels, "It is safe to assume that shelter from inclement weather, protection from predatory neighbors (human or otherwise), and comfort and privacy for family life, were the chief reasons which impelled men in the first instance to live in houses." This assumption was also behind Unwin's desire to establish edges between town and country and his growing admiration for medieval and baroque city gates and walls. His conviction that the human need to withdraw or feel familiar and secure ought to be sustained more than the instinct to expand, adventure, or move out, explains a great deal of the character of his thought and desires at this time. Altogether it offered a way to reduce the fright of modern scale and unlimited space.

For those who take Parker and Unwin's praise of simplicity and purity at face value, it comes as a surprise to notice how the architects occasionally complicate the essential form of a house scheme, with a bay projecting here, an inglenook or porch indenting there, roofs and chimneys breaking down into all sorts of minor silhouettes and planes. The built-in and repetitive furniture they featured tended to intensify this effect in the smaller space inside. One explanation for this is that, in their view, everything had to have a demonstrable public reason: form was following function down to the minutest detail. Another factor was that no matter how far Parker, especially, seems to have gone toward stylistic Purism, there was always a reminiscence of the earlier Japanese print, *art nouveau,* or Pre-

Raphaelite mannerism in his work. He was a real child of his times. What difference this can make is easily recognized if one studies for comparison the puristic private houses of Voysey, Baillie Scott, or Frank Lloyd Wright, which are complicated enough but not so thoroughly analyzed or self-consciously rational in every detail and facet, and so catch up a more relaxed, consistent, independent, and lyrical rhythm. Essentially, however, it appears fair as well as accurate to interpret Parker and Unwin's publicly conscientious houses and towns as forms within forms, as frames within frames, as crystals within crystals, for spatial control and overall rather than singular protection. It follows from their old theme of a full development and nurture of the individual for the collective good.

One of the most durable of these enclaving forms was the quadrangle. They discussed it many times but only achieved it in quantity at Hampstead Garden Suburb, beginning in 1906. The ideogram of the quad again goes back to Unwin's youth in Oxford and to William Morris and his idea of the kind of life that should be encouraged within it, particularly to his adult education centers in great country houses.

The provision of communal laundries and baths with playrooms adjoining in the quad relates to a number of mid-century and earlier dreams, such as those of Robert Owen, but it also foreshadows Unwin's pioneer insistence upon indoor plumbing for even the humblest dwelling, which was turned into law. This relates further to his concern with the cost of utilities in the street, which ultimately led to an effort to cut the number, length, and width of streets so as to reduce the investment in pipes and paving for single house units while widening the frontage (Fig. 48). This view is prominently displayed in the booklet, *Nothing Gained by Overcrowding!* of 1912. But the arresting thing is how quickly one item or conclusion could follow another in Unwin's thought process, sometimes canceling, sometimes compensating. In one way he was most remarkable in that he was the eternal amateur. Even when he became the most knowledgeable man in the western world for planning, full of statistics and comparative studies, and called by *The New York Times* the "internationally known dean of town planners and housing experts," or by the British Town Planning Institute the "Head of

19

Fig. 1   Raymond Unwin as a young man.   Fig. 2   Unwin as a middle-aged man.

Fig. 3   Unwin as an older man.

In youth and middle age there is keenness and drive in the face. With advanced age the wisdom comes forth. Insofar as he typified generations and decades he was at first the individualistic reform artist of the 1890's and finally in the 1930's the kind, confident technician and administrator, which that decade needed so sadly.

the Planning Profession for men of all countries," he is still at pains to make it evident that he is as baffled by what cities are really all about as any layman. He urges students to use intuition as well as the behavioral sciences as tools, and to be ever alert to the psychology of the populations they are dealing with. In the next breath, however, he typically tells them they do not need to keep up on specific complexes or any of that other "jargon," as he terms it, that accumulates under the heading of professional psychology. He held tenaciously to the common-sense, common touch, even when dealing with problems of surrealistic dimensions. His own intellect was remarkable enough, but never so that you would notice it if he could help it. His portraits have a gentle, bland, tweedy, folksy, quality about them, but, particularly in profile, one also detects the quick, hawklike determination and will power (Figs. 1, 2, 3), and always around the eyes, the steady intelligence.

TOWN PLANNING IN PRACTICE, 1909

The four-hundred page book from the end of Unwin's more private career is *Town Planning in Practice.* He anticipated with it the Housing and Town Planning Act of 1909, sponsored by John Burns, who had also helped him to have passed the Hampstead Garden Suburb Act of 1906, which restored the legality of the outlawed cul-de-sac or close of the earlier nineteenth century. Unconsciously Unwin may have been anticipating his debut into full-time government service in 1914. Among other features, the 1909 act provided for the limitation of the density, height, and character of buildings.

Hence it is something of a how-to-do-it book. Yet it had a new dimension too, a more independent, cosmopolitan, and widely traveled air. He discerns the informal beauty of many European medieval cities but advises that they should not be repeated verbatim. The German system, although it had taken advantage of new planning powers more effectively than England, France, or America, appears under the guidance of its architects to have gone too far in imitating medieval precedent. He recognizes the American grid and the persuasion that it is the cheapest and most efficient layout for a city. In later years when he knows the United States better, he takes

21

this assumption up again and examines it more rigorously, attempting then to demonstrate that the opposite is more likely the actuality.

Public spaces and streets are treated for the first time in his writing as a large and separate interest, bringing in some features from the influence of Camillo Sitte's *Der Städtebau* of 1889. In the first chapter it is evident that he is not going to settle for improved building codes, fire protection, and sanitation, which were understood by most to be the substantive reforms of the last quarter of the nineteenth century and to need but a little adjustment. He declares, "It is the lack of beauty, of the amenities of life, more than anything else which obliges us to admit that our work of town building in the last century has not been well done." The last decade of the nineteenth century made it inevitable that he and his contemporaries use the terms "civic art" or "civic design" when referring to what nowadays would be broadly called in America "city planning" and in Britain "town planning," or, more narrowly, "urban design." Yet he declared that it was a "pattern of life" he was seeking more than any form of "civic design," as such. So he says, "civic art must be the expression of the life of the community," and actually means it. The full build-up of a community interplay on the initiative of its citizens constantly in touch with each other would be civic art to him. Art had a sociological and behavioral silhouette and body. Because the nineteenth-century environment had expanded so alarmingly during the 1870's and 1880's, as he noted in his acceptance speech of the gold medal of the Royal Institute of British Architects in 1937, he had been early forced to the conclusion that a new physical order was demanded. An improved physical appearance thus ought to express an inner virtue and integrity as well as become an outer cover for society. Perhaps this conception had something to do with his constant search for abstract and geometric formulas into which a new order could be fitted. Beauty was to be introduced for two causes: to slow down change to the point where it would have an enduring rather than a transient effect (unlike a style) and to demonstrate, visibly and externally, once and for all, that an internal order of society was possible. Unwin had no final or underlying hostility to bylaw streets, and to the better sanitation and lighting, of the last half of the nineteenth century. He merely wished to improve more substantially on the improvements. The international historic sequence is obvious in his development: the urban confusion and anarchy of the 1870's and 1880's and then the succeeding aspirations toward beauty and order of the 1890's (known unpopularly now in the United States as the "City Beautiful" movement of Daniel Burnham and Charles McKim) with the impulse tapering off after 1900 and up to World War I into suburban and country domestic work of a more open, plain, quiet, and refined sort. Parker and Unwin conformed to this evolution stylistically, but they were unique in widening and developing it into regional planning and for constantly watching out for interlocking details, how one part might authentically relate to the other. In this sense they were truly "organic" architects and planners, for it is the identifying of complicated relationships within a community which supports the connotation of "organic" better than any Darwinian conception that it is analogous to a human or animal body, or even a plant. For instance, when Unwin calls attention to the fact that the bylaw "better" streets can cost £3 per yard in frontage in contrast to the worth of £200 or less per cottage, and that this tends to narrow frontages unmercifully (Fig. 11), a new association of cause and effect is gained that many city officials and subdividers have yet to perceive. The expense of utilities and streets, as well as the necessity for large numbers of vehicles to move rapidly about in the larger nineteenth-century city, tended to reduce the intrinsic value of location as a place to stop at and live in. It was his and his partner's vigorous promotion of a graded network of major and minor, paved and unpaved, wide and narrow streets that led to the invention both of the cul-de-sac and the secondary and service road: as one comes closer to the home, as in Hampstead, he is slowed down by narrower and shorter roads. The length of house frontage with them was always related to the cost of paving and utilities. But in interpreting Parker and Unwin's therapy, it is important to remember that no one factor or answer can ever outweigh or dominate the others entirely, except possibly the modulus of beauty. The indispensable element for the achievement of beauty was a balance among all these factors. To put it in a little different and more personal light, as Sir Frederic Osborn has said, "Unwin's is a cardinal name in planning and housing history, because he combined three distinguished qualities—proficiency as a technician, sociological insight, and the ability to explain." All that is missing in this summation of Unwin's balance is the aesthetic initiative pervading in his mind from Ruskin and Morris.

NOTHING GAINED BY OVERCROWDING! 1912

The pamphlet *Nothing Gained by Overcrowding!* was prepared for the Garden Cities and Town Planning Association and published in 1912. Again, it is tractarian in character, as had been the pamphlet *Cottage Plans and Common Sense* of a decade before for the gradualist Fabian Society. It exhibits a bias toward garden city principles and the 1909 Town Planning Act. More than being disordered, the modern city was an amorphous, shapeless mass, Unwin explained again, as he had in *Town Planning in Practice*. Earlier his invention had tended to center around smaller devices and shorter lines. Now there was a reactive shift in scale to more basic problem solving, animated finally by the emergence of the big, basic superform. There was also a renewed interest in what has endurance in an elastic and highly dynamic situation. Instead of simplicity of design, simplicity of concept or diagram was to be given greater emphasis. The huge, all-inclusive solution is sought because it promises so much more return from a limited investment. The abstract was also supposed to encompass the enlarging actuality more efficiently, quickly, and easily (Fig. 29). In "Higher Building in Relation to Town Planning" Unwin advises that the planner "must depend on his trained imagination to keep the forest as a whole ever clearly in his view while his mind is occupied threading its way through the obstructing trees and their distracting shadows. If he misses the one simple and direct path to unity, which when found will appear to all to have been quite obvious, he will usually have produced not a design at all, but a mere compilation." As with the idiom of common sense, it was the fresh and unjaded viewpoint that he found most rewarding. Unwin had noticed about the planner, shortly before, that "perhaps there is something unusual in his make-up which predisposes him, with childlike innocence, to put more faith than some of his neighbours in the simple and the obvious." There was a Seurat-like directness in his thought (Fig. 5), an Alice-in-Wonderland marveling (Fig. 6), and a Morris-like, adolescent yearning for a new vitality and energy of social pattern evolving from nature and tradition (Fig. 7). All these views did appear elementary and naïve to later generations in one way or another and at one time or another, but not in the idealistic way Unwin originally intended.

Fig. 4   The Parker and Unwin families, c. 1899. At the right is Unwin and on his knee his son, Edward, named for Edward Carpenter. Just behind them is his wife, Ethel, sister of Barry Parker, his partner, who stands above. Keeping the connection and integrity of the family was one of the special goals of Parker and Unwin.

Fig. 5 "Une Baignade," Georges Seurat, 1883–1884.

Fig. 6 "Alice and the White Rabbit," John Tenniel, 1866.

26

Fig. 7   Norwich Wallpaper, William Morris, 1889.

In the artworks of the 1880's, the formative decade for Unwin, already can be discerned problems with which he will have to deal later. The rival scale between Alice and the White Rabbit, with her head against the ceiling, is comparable to the contrast in the urban environment between factories, chimneys, gas works, viaducts and railroad stations (and later apartments and skyscrapers) with houses. One bit of mushroom made the city grow bigger, another caused the houses and people to shrink, but they were compelled to remain in the same ambient as the city demanded first more labor and then more service.

In the Seurat painting, items are also related, but in a curiously numbed, anonymous and quick frozen way. People become tantamount to objects and a disturbing loneliness in close proximity develops as these young men try to find recreation and commune with nature within sight of each other and factory chimneys and smoke. Their backs turn. Their faces are muted.

In Unwin's work this proximate question and the suggested solution appear most conspicuously in Hampstead Garden Suburb near London. In the Morris wallpaper is the older Victorian and British instinct to bring incongruous elements into a meaningful pattern, to cause them to interrelate, harmonize, and count from a distance. The vigor was inherent from the nature of the society and time; the harmony was not. This required the artist. Unwin likened good planning sometimes to music, more often to wallpaper, or a textile. He knew and wrote for Morris. He spoke of his own underlying purpose as one of forming "a pattern of life." The abstract formulation of Morris wallpaper, the microform, was transmuted by Unwin during the course of his career into the huge abstraction of the regional plan connected by throughways, the metropolis with its satellite cities, the superforms, which, like Seurat's figures, were supposed to maintain their individuality and integrity by the separation of greenbelts—entities in sight but not touching, keeping their distance.

27

On looking down on his plans of this period, it is evident that he is more and more measuring the distances and relations among objects. He takes the cottage (which must be small and inexpensive) and argues for a green space around it as the best possible compensating investment for the well-being of the family. The simpler house with more land follows the same line of reasoning as fewer streets in a more open community. They were putting their money where their minds were in spending on the latter two items while working out economies for the former two. He goes on to recommend houses in clusters of two, four, and six units, shaped in T's, U's, and squares so that they could be wrapped about cul-de-sacs or greens at the end of his special short roads, for which he succeeded in having passed his special Hampstead law of 1906. Always there is a need to congregate, to assemble, to bring people together and arrange them properly, to form "a queue rather than a crowd."

His ultimate diagrammatic enclosure was the great circle. It was supposed to contain a full radioconcentric city, most notably London (Fig. 28, 29, 38, 39). The assumption was that the further out from the center the settlements were to be made, the more inhabitants could be accommodated. The geometry of the situation, as Unwin described it, was that "the area of a circle increases not in proportion to the distance from the centre to the circumference but in proportion to the square of that distance." This leaves the inhabitants still within comfortable commuting time of the center *if* proper transport can be supplied and the community efficiently distributed internally. The huge, simple, circular forms he evolves for his satellite or federated cities revert toward Ebenezer Howard's similar geometric diagrams, which previously had appeared so anachronistic and out of the 1850's.

Yet while elements were being drawn together and rationally arranged in theory, the land was beginning in actuality to be freed to flow out, and usually downward, among his buildings. This is particularly evident when he is writing of city squares and the need of a view out to the landscape from inside the town. To reduce the population of London theoretically from 64 to 42 per acre would be for the purpose of realistically settling the surplus at 25 per acre in outer and greater London and in the countryside. To allow no more

28

than twelve houses per acre would equitably balance off the return on land with the development cost of extra roads and facilities. Although "twelve to the acre" was a highly significant slogan among garden city enthusiasts and was actually woven into the law (for Unwin recognized the law, too, as a highly creative instrument), it was often misunderstood and far from invulnerable. Parker let the game go when he admitted it was largely a rule of thumb, which sought to engage the relatively low cost of land at the instant it surpassed the relatively high cost of roads, water supply, surface water drains, sewer, gas, etc. Unwin claimed that land of high value was only "local" but the local power and magnetism of nodal or treasure spots when placed in great cities under the rising pressure of urban populations was great indeed. In this respect he and Parker were trying to move against a major trend following the industrial and urban revolutions. He had to admit also that a single owner could squeeze or "sweat" a single small parcel of land and still come out far ahead. In theory he wished to make a rule binding on all whereby the equity of value potential would be more evenly spaced with no congestion or great pressure points. This caused him and his partner to look avidly as their careers advanced for larger sources of capital with which to buy bigger quantities of land and to carry out wider and longer range building programs, especially after the experience at Letchworth, where the vision never quite materialized because they were so often desperately short of cash at the very period they were creating future capital through a more amenable environment. It also caused Barry Parker and the management of Welwyn Garden City to have a higher regard for architectural control and to gravi- tate, between the two wars, toward regional and national planning. Yet the final British longing is not for a rudimentary scheme, a single perfectly brilliant solution, a "crystal" like a diamond, but for a modeled and muted landscape, a beautiful, rich, green, undulating, continuous land sculpture with the buildings set companionably into it. The geometric diagram was the theoretical resolution, looking splendid on paper, but the conviction that steady testing in the field was the only source of fundamental strength to be conserved for posterity through the further development of a landscape tradition was the more persistent aim. This motivation was somewhat moral and literary as with the American utopians, it was somewhat abstract and philosophical as with the European idealists, but its real distinction lay in the willingness to work with the means at hand and the acknowledgment that it might take decades to reach the millenium.

"HIGHER BUILDING IN RELATION TO
TOWN PLANNING," 1924

After the first war it was a different world. However, the paths of Unwin's interest continued to move in the same direction. During visits to New York, he was intrigued by the skyscrapers going up. The bad effects of these, which he suggested as potential for London, were largely pooh-poohed by his English audience, and the most unfortunate results did not, indeed, appear in London until after World War II. The saturation point for automotive traffic was not in view, but already in Chicago it was a big problem and likely to get bigger, he noted (Fig. 36). His previous interest in major planning brought him into communication again with Thomas Adams, who had been the secretary of Letchworth Garden City and was presently occupied with a regional study of New York City for the Russell Sage Foundation (1922–1931). Henry Wright, with the encouragement of Clarence Stein and Lewis Mumford, had been working on a plan for the whole state of New York, to be incorporated in a report to Governor Al Smith. It was on Wright's death in the summer of 1936 that Unwin was invited to Columbia University. The superform and superplan in this country were rapidly becoming something both to conjure with and face. Unwin had observed as early as 1910 in connection with the Burnham plans that "a grasp and breadth of treatment of the whole [city] question" was America at its best. Now he wanted to examine it at its worst.

In "Higher Building in Relation to Town Planning," printed in the Journals of the Royal Institute of British Architects and the American Institute of Architects, he improvises one of his characteristic diagrams to show how pedestrians and cars would appear in the streets if the skyscrapers were abruptly emptied of their occupants, as during a five o'clock rush (Fig. 32). Despite the absence of skyscrapers in England, the situation provoked many of the troublesome issues he was skilled in dramatizing: the dense coverage of land, too many and wide streets, the absence of sunshine and ventilation, the clustering of abstract forms and the subsequent reduction of the voids which served them, the negative working and living conditions for people. He indicated that one had to consider these buildings not only in terms of horizontal bus transport, but also of the vertical elevator, and how long it took to move with one system as opposed to another, or into one from the other. His English sensitivity to time appears to have enabled him to recognize the essence of the great American problem of time versus space almost at once.

He maintained that the American street grid stalled the traffic at intersections. It was too uniform from north to south, east to west. Forty percent of the area of downtown Chicago was already in streets, he said. The wider thoroughfares were obstructive because main artery traffic was held up for the crossing of pedestrians and the fewer vehicles from the less used side streets. The battle to properly time stop lights had already begun, and an arresting footnote to traffic history appears in the fact that green originally meant "stop" and white "go!"

In contrast to Berenice Abbott, with her remarkable photographs of Lower Manhattan, unlike the painter John Marin, who had returned to the United States just before the war from Paris to try to capture in dramatic water color the dynamism of this same area, unlike Georgia O'Keeffe, who painted views of skyscrapers like the Radiator Building and the Shelton Hotel during the mid-1920's as single and supposedly ascendant symbols of a brave new postwar world, Unwin chose the Woolworth Building as an instance of a form to be avoided, at all costs, if ever a postwar boom happened again. The fourteen thousand workers in it would require a mile and a quarter of sidewalk if strolling, or 2,800 feet if standing and packed closely (Fig. 33). Assuming the average of U.S. car ownership at the time, one for every ten people, their automobiles would require 4,200 feet of idling room or a ribbon of six or seven miles were their owners to drive them to work. He used photographs of the evening or morning rush to suggest the depressing mood of the great canyons of stone with the shadows slanting low and the debris blowing through them (Figs. 34, 60).

"REGIONAL PLANNING WITH SPECIAL REFERENCE TO LONDON," 1930

Raymond Unwin employs the terms "site" and "regional plan" as equivalents now, and the weight is more upon proof of the permanent benefit than the transitory or speculative worth of the land. He observes very generally here, "the [design] principle applies to parts of a pattern traced on a flat background; to the grouping of walls, roofs and windows into a façade; to the disposition of buildings and openings around a civic center, or to the laying down of a pattern for distributing urban development over the undulating background of hill and dale, field and forest, forming the region."

The utility of Unwin's genius as it relates to the twentieth century seems to derive from the interchangeability of the instruments of his philosophy, ranging from a geometric diagram covering hundreds of square miles to a single site layout taking careful advantage of every five-foot contour, down to a minuscule wallpaper or a textile pattern, which he sometimes preferred to use to describe what he was seeking in terms of a visual concept. This is one way we know for sure he began with William Morris (Fig. 7). The language is always visual and pictorial, no matter what the medium or the purpose.

Unwin went further than other designers and social reformers (including Ruskin, Morris and Geddes) in turning to officialdom as a critical agency for refashioning the land. This piece deals also with the need to lift regional committees from their advisory role to one having a really coordinating, although not necessarily originating, power.

Altogether Unwin wanted to get over the nightmare of haphazard and sporadic settlement made possible by the outthrust of the railroad, rapid transit, and later, and more unfortunately, the car. With him it was not overspill evenly around the rim, but overslop, oversplash, widely scattered ink blots, that confused and debilitated (Fig. 38). His own decentralization was instead to be a consistent and logical thinning, inside the city limits and out. The discriminating lovers of greenery who could afford it had disengaged themselves from the late nineteenth- and early twentieth-century city and fled further and further out into the country. A distinguished early example of this was Bedford Park, as he says in this article, connected to London by rail. Now the mob began to pursue them relentlessly with automobile and bus, logical vehicles driven out at random via an over-elaborate network of highways and streets rather than radially along steel tracks or electric lines. Unwin's first proposal for London was to concentrate the activities of commerce and administration in the giant central core. The distraction of secondary activities generated by "crowds engaged in unimportant details, such as the purchase of gramaphone records, or the passing to and from the hatter to the tailor," would disappear. The central area would be redeveloped with residences for those who serviced the important administrative work, who belonged there by virtue of their function as decision and contract makers. Multiples of four to six thousand population would then take up the outside: self-contained, crystallographic, satellite towns, with plenty of green recreational and amenity space to be kept among them (Fig. 39). The theme of the New Towns, fully discussed during the 1920's and '30's but only to be realized after World War II, was about to have its overture.

The parkway or throughway with secondary service roads, introduced into Britain in the late 1920's by Barry Parker at Wythenshawe and based on American models, should be the means of communicating between these new towns. The "art of planning" was to bring "the science of urban development" into "such appropriate relations and good proportions that a coherent whole will be created, and will combine the many developments into a design on the background of open land, harmonizing, with the nature of the site. Thus there may be given at least the opportunity for a beautiful environment, out of which a good human life may grow." This seems a harmless enough exhortation, but for future city planners it had about as radical an implication as if political "scientists" were abruptly called upon to rename themselves political "artists," or as if doctors were to be henceforth described only as "healers."

By now Unwin was a very accomplished technician as well as a bold theorist. But no matter how intricate the problem or how sophisticated or all embracing his proposals, he never outgrew his confidence in and human affection for open space and the land, his faith in beauty as a positive element in human affairs, his expectation that a planner should be committed and concerned, a social artist before he was a social scientist, *and,* above all, that he should not lose his head, should have common sense.

HOUSING AND TOWN PLANNING LECTURES AT COLUMBIA UNIVERSITY, 1936–1937, 1938–1939

In reviewing the Columbia Lectures, two underlying conditions of the period have to be recalled. Carl Feiss in his brief introduction to the 1936–1937 series describes them (and through them, of course, Unwin himself) as exceptional in their directness and simplicity of style. Surrounding the intrinsic simplicity of these lectures, as of Unwin's life, has to be imagined the lowering grey veil of the depression in Britain and the United States and the threatening gloom of an oncoming war. His last years must have been particularly difficult because the international rapport and aspiration he represented in being past president of the International Housing and Town Planning Association, and in his promotion of the League of Nations, appeared about to be completely negated. Yet, as he noted in his first lecture, it always had been hard for him to credit the Malthusian theory of too many people for too few resources. Such pessimism merely inhibited progress and constructive thinking. An air of optimism and a mental shrug were more natural to him. He had seen things change for the better and had helped them come about. It would be impossible to read these gentle lectures only and realize that Unwin was in his middle seventies and not far from death, that the kind of world in which he had so long believed appeared about to crumble, and that he had once moved mountains and would no doubt like to do so again.

Perhaps the greatest lesson to be learned from these talks is of patient courage, for, as Unwin says himself, he is not completely conversant with American conditions, and the students would have to depend upon Mr. Feiss and the rest of the staff for that.

The other prevailing attitude is Unwin's touching eagerness to explain to students how necessary it is not to lose hope or meaningful touch with the best traditions of the past. Essentially, he himself is now a voice out of the past, but it is his view that the past still has much to tell, even to students and New Yorkers. Later events have proved his attitudes and intuitions less transitory than the crises which were then swirling about them and the other things he most dearly loved. In simplest terms, individual good judgment and character might yet be the qualities most needed and depended upon by the corporate and fast changing society. In his last lecture in March 1939, entitled "State and National Planning," he says, "Psychological judgment of how large numbers of folk will act, and what the economic reactions of change may be, may become as, or even more, important than, technical knowledge of physical planning. None the less, whatever the range, planning involves the formation of a fresh conception of the relations to be established between the parts, whether that conception is more or less visual in character. The training of the planner to concentrate his thought and his visualizing imagination on relations, rather than on the details of the parts to be related, commencing with a few relations in a limited area and expanding to more and more as the area grows, is probably one of the best approaches to planning in any sphere and to any extent. As, however, the volume of knowledge needed soon exceeds the powers of any individual, close cooperation on the part of those more skilled and experienced in the economic and social spheres, with the physical planner who is to express the new conception in the environment, seems essential. The work of the National Resources Committee in the U.S.A. affords perhaps the most valuable material available for the study of scope and method in National Planning." These comments are to some degree a summation of Unwin's own odyssey. As an artist and a young man he was in conflict with conventional society, but unlike so many of his contemporaries who grew bitter, stiff, and frustrated with advancing age and new disappointment, Unwin merely took on more and more responsibility. Instead of trying to defend in depth a highly personal and exclusive vision, as an artist he endeavored to make his life a demonstration that the vision was an elemental and all-inclusive one and that he was forever ready to share it with others. His final teaching was that something *could* be done by a teacher, Shaw to the contrary.

"LAND VALUES IN RELATION TO PLANNING AND HOUSING IN THE UNITED STATES," 1941

In this last article, printed after his death, Unwin tries again to bring the rapid growth in the urban United States to the intellectual boiling point, to a state of brightest clarity where the really operative forces would be at last revealed to all. His constant attention to the land and his awareness of the theories of the American Henry George would cause him to be additionally alert to this situation. However, he believes the cessation of immigration, the decline of natural increase in population, and the depression in America caused certain urban values tied to municipal tax systems and great expectations to be artificially maintained and therefore extremely doubtful. There was a shortage in the supply of value around the central business district in the gray area with a great oversupply within the center itself. Inflation or overpricing was occurring in the wrong spots. "Where land is not used or where buildings are not occupied, no actual value is being created, and no real land value exists." Much of Unwin's statistical argument was based on Homer Hoyt's well-known study of Chicago and New York real estate values of the past century.

Unwin reiterated his earlier scheme for the decentralization of London within a smaller compass by proposing that houses be placed directly in the gray areas so as to absorb the surplus land more rapidly. "Consequently the low density must mean for the city a higher total of land value, and a more stable tax basis, whereas high density reduces the total land value and greatly increases the degree of uncertainty as to tax revenues."

This posthumous essay, carefully edited by Carl Feiss, is more amply furnished with supplementary information and footnotes than Unwin's usual articles. And it has no pictures or diagrams. Thus we sense that Unwin himself must have gone. Yet, as his Columbia Lectures showed great courage on the downward path, so this last, posthumous, exertion conveys the inevitable common sense to illustrate how nonsensical, how Alice-like, the twentieth century American city could be and again, almost like a fading echo, comes the reassuring message that there is no need to be overawed by the city, in spite of its gigantic size and power. We read for the last time that the truly great opportunities for synthesis should be sought out by and stored up in the human mind and spirit.

CONCLUSION

It appeared all along unlikely that Unwin's answers could attain a permanent validity in a situation that altered as rapidly as that of the first half of the twentieth century. The most significant act seems rather the continued framing and putting of penetrating questions to his own and following generations.

George Bernard Shaw wrote to the son of Sir Ebenezer Howard on the latter's death in 1928, "He was one of those heroic simpletons who do big things whilst our prominent worldlings are explaining why they are Utopian and impossible." This apparently callous summation of Unwin's major client for the first garden city might be charitably applied to Unwin himself. Indeed, in his papers he kept a quotation from Ruskin with the following underlined, "And this blind and cowardly spirit is forever telling you that . . . good things are impossible, and you need not live for them." He too was at first glance a little simple, a little naïve, a little childish, and he liked the idea. Children, after all, ask interesting questions.

On the other hand, when the dimensions of the conflicts with which he had to cope are recognized, he does not appear quite so simple. A deep-dyed individualist and rebel at heart, a strong champion of the underdog, as his partner always said, an artist, and a hero worshipper, he never allowed his mind or imagination to wander off the reservation, to cut out on him or his society. He learned to live and act within the actual environment and possibilities which surrounded him, devilishly inconsistent and illogical as they might sometimes appear to be. He heroically got whole towns built and difficult laws passed. He founded and was president of several professional societies of international significance. He advised great governments and spoke and taught at famous universities.

37

He loved "pure design" and the beauty of nature as much or more than anyone, but he would not allow these passions to blind him to the equal importance of economics, law, or social psychology. A responsible person of great good will and stature in the Victorian sense becomes so much more rare by the early twentieth century and after World War I that his reputation is still being, and no doubt will continue to be, alternately lost and found. Yet, as the model village led into the garden village, and the garden village to the garden city, and the garden city to the new and satellite towns, there is also a thread in Unwin's practice and thought as represented by his writing that may be altogether golden: it may show that ideas, even in the modern age when stretched against overwhelming odds and put under excruciating pressures, can have a cumulative worth, a tensile strength, a compressive resistance, and a great human durability; that true innovation and revolution in the science of planning may consist in discovering what to save and remember, as well as what to originate in each generation; indeed, that they are legitimately part of the same process.

I

Quotations
Cherished by Unwin

Quotations from earlier artists and authors which Raymond Unwin kept among his papers and which seem to have deeply influenced him. He appears to have known each of them personally, except Millet. The italics are Unwin's.

CARPENTER, EDWARD (1844–1929)
Art is expression: expression of that which is else inexpressible. In all true art, wherever we see beauty, something passes to us, some touch of that which is infinite: something from a kindred soul to ours. Architecture, painting, music, in each a miracle; bricks and mortar, smeared pigments, and air vibrations becoming alive. The identical essential and continual miracle of creation or nature.

LETHABY, W. R. (1857–1931)
Little in ancient architecture was "designed." Things designed by a single mind are mostly "sports," which must quickly perish. Only that which is in the line of development can persist. . . .

. . . .

An expressive form of art is only reached by building out in one direction during a long time. No art that is only one man deep is worth much; it should be a thousand men deep.

. . . .

To forget the past would be as foolish as to ignore the future. Behind is custom, as in front is adventure.

. . . .

The ability to make is a form of Culture as well as the ability to talk and producing no less honorable than consuming.

CHAPTER ONE

To me work is not only Art, but it is almost everything else as well.

.   .   .   .

Be all this as it may, a new and better London can only be completed as Old Rome was founded by turning a plough trench round about it.

MILLET, J. F. (1814–1875)

One may say *that everything is beautiful provided the thing turns up in its own place;* and contrariwise that nothing can be beautiful arriving inappropriately. Let Apollo *be* Apollo, and Socrates Socrates. Which is the more beautiful a straight tree or a crooked tree? Whichever is the most in place. This then is my conclusion *The Beautiful is that which is in place.*

MORRIS, WILLIAM (1834–1896)

While it lasted, everything that was made by man was adorned by man, *just as everything made by nature is adorned by her.* The craftsman, as he fashioned the thing he had under his hand, ornamented it so naturally and so entirely without conscious effort, *that it is often difficult to distinguish where the mere utilitarian part of his work ended and the ornamental began.* Now the *origin of this art was the necessity that the workman felt for variety in his work,* and *though the beauty produced by this desire was a great gift to the world, yet the obtaining variety and pleasure in the work by the workman was a matter of more* importance still, for it stamped all labour with the impress of pleasure.

.   .   .   .

Then a man shall work and bethink him, and rejoice in the deeds of his hand.

.   .   .   .

We must turn this land from the grimy back yard of a workshop into a garden. If that seems difficult I cannot help it; I only know that it is necessary.

RUSKIN, JOHN (1819–1900)

Architecture is the art which so disposes and adorns the edifices raised by man, for whatsoever uses, that the sight of them may contribute to his mental health, power, and pleasure.

.   .   .   .

Let every dawn of morning be to you as the beginning of life, and every setting sun be to you as its close:—then let every one of these short lives leave its sure record of some kindly thing done for others —some goodly strength or knowledge gained for yourselves; so, from day to day, and strength to strength, you shall build up indeed, by Art, by Thought, and by Just Will, an Ecclesia of England, of which it shall not be said, 'See what manner of stones are here,' but, 'See what manner of men.'

2

"The Dawn of a Happier Day"

Manchester, January 1886. Written in faded brown ink in a difficult hand in a magenta exercise book, when Unwin was twenty-two, this essay, which appears never to have been published, deals mainly with conditions of labor and class.

THE wants and comforts which are conducive to a happy life are comparatively few. A house to live in, furniture, clothes, food, some books and a few works of art about comprise the list. Is it possible that with all the increase in our powers of production through the use of machinery, steam and other agents, we cannot easily supply every member of the community with these without burdening him with more than a healthy amount of labour? Let us see what William Hoyle says on the matter. He has carefully studied this question and finds that on the average one man will produce enough food for twenty at least, and clothing for fifty; and he estimates the amount of labour needed to supply our houses and furniture at about the same as food. To one man with hours 20 say; then the amount of labour needed to provide for our wants will be every day, for food half an hour, clothing quarter of an hour, house and furniture half an hour; a total of 1 to 4 hours labour a day, supposing each to do his share, would keep us all in the comforts of life. This leaves a large margin for extension without encroaching on any one's love of leisure; for assuming that each had to work four hours a day at some useful work either of head or hand who would be the worse for it? Would not our refined claims be much the better for four hours daily of really practical work of some sort and would not our working classes have a much better chance of becoming more refined under such conditions of work than under the present?

It is only when we have learned to cooperate for our common needs that there will be the chance for all of sharing the enobling influence of honorably earned leisure, of study, art and science. Only then will the beauties of nature be open to every one, and will it be possible for every child to spend more of its summers digging in the sands by the seaside, for every man so inclined to roam over the hills and valleys of our country and learn to revere nature. To the vast majority such treats are confined to a Whitmonday excursion if got at all and there are still to be found people living in our large towns who have never seen a clear stream.

Under such a system of cooperative work we shall soon learn to judge of the values of things in something approaching a real and true manner. There will be no temptation to make cheap and nasty goods, because there will be no profit to be got by so doing. If any one wants work doing which is in itself unpleasant and necessary he will have to do it himself or try to do without it or bribe some one else with a high rate of pay, for there will be no class of men out of work ready to do any sort of work for a living. Every man will be able to work at some trade suitable to him and as soon as it is found that there are more workers than there is work the hours will be reduced, for while there are wants unsupplied there will be always work, and as soon as there are no wants unsupplied the hours of labour can be reduced without any one going short of a needed comfort.

In fact this system of work which Socialists wish to see established will be able to put happiness within the reach of all so far as happiness is the result of, or in any way depends on circumstances.

And here let us look at one or two objections to this scheme. First it is often said that we shall reduce all to a dead level and subject every one to a tyranny of endless officialism. It is thought that association must tend to crush out individuality. There is no doubt that there must be discipline in our work, each will not be able to do what seems right in his own eyes, at least not while at work; and here we must notice that it is certain that whatever time is found by experience to be necessary it will be a vast deal less than at present probably our assumption of 4 hours is exceedingly safe, so that even granting a very great amount of officialism and a great anti-individual force during the hours of work, they would be too short for it to have any great evil effect on our lives and the time which will be absolutely at our own disposal will be so long that there will be every

43

chance for individual development. Nor must we in imagining difficulties which may and doubtless will arise under a Socialist system of production lose sight of the fact that our present system is so far from perfect in fact that for many thousands of the workers it would be impossible to make it worse. Any one who has worked in a mill or ironworks will know that there is no lack of officialism now; a boss who considers himself a sort of superior animal, who feels quite at liberty to air his whims regardless of the trouble they cause to the workers can be quite as unpleasant as any official and probably much more so than any officials needed in a socialist organization.

Another objection often urged is that we shall find the people as a whole will not know how to pay men of science, men of thought, musicians, poets or artists. Here again one must first remember that many of the greatest men—poets, artists, scientists, have gone to the grave unpaid under our present system and it is frequently only the succeeding generations who have learnt to honour them. Thus the best work is not done for money but for the love of doing it, and our socialist community will at least do this, it will enable every man to earn his own living without taking up any of the time he may wish to devote to science or the arts. And without entering into the question whether a man can expect to reap a reward in wealth, who does the deeds of art of science of poetry or music, we may fairly trust I think to the community to see that its great men are rewarded, and to provide for all those who are devoting their time to investigating truth for the benefit of mankind especially as any neglect on their part will only entail a few hours work daily on the one neglected.

It is quite certain that honour will not be wanting to disinterested workers for the common good, any more than it is wanting in the army with deeds of bravery; a man will be respected for what he does for the community, not for what he gets for himself.

3

"Gladdening v. Shortening the Hours of Labour"

A handwritten speech to the Sheffield Socialist Education League, February 1, 1897. Sheffield was not only a center of labor unrest in the North, but also the focus for the utopian handicraft colonies of John Ruskin and Edward Carpenter, two of Unwin's earliest idols.

CONSIDER then if we increase largely our leisure what shall we do with it, how increase our happiness. Games are already pushed to such an extent that they become professions, trades another form of work. It seems that we must look to hobbies to fill our spare time with happiness. We must anticipate that the increase of leisure will lead to a large increase of amateur work, work that is which is undertaken for the love of the work or of the result of the work. Men will take more to gardening, they are already doing so as witness the allotment movement, they will take to growing their own fruit, vegetables for the sake partly of the work and interest and partly for the result. They will take to carpentering and cabinet work and will make their own furniture and some for their friends, they will take to making their own shoes, their own clothes, they will take to working in iron or brass and some will take to the artistic handicrafts. Now what will be the difference between the work so done and the ordinary task work by which men earn their wages? First their hearts will be in it, they will enjoy it, then they will do it thoroughly well to the best of their power and knowledge, no one takes pleasure in doing work badly it is the doing of it well and thoroughly that brings satisfaction largely. Then too they will take an intelligent interest in it. If a man is making a pair of shoes for his wife or for a friend he will think of the foot the shoe has to fit—of the life that man leads and in what circumstances the shoe will be worn

45

and so will try to make the shoe as comfortable as possible and as durable. A man making shoes by the gross has no such interest in his work, no human relationship in it whatever, nothing he is lead to think of but how many he can make and how much he can earn in a given length of time. Then too amateur work develops beauty of work. The man who works for the pleasure and interest of it will naturally think of the look of all he makes, he will wish to express his pleasure in the thing he makes, he will think of it, at all times notice beautiful examples he may see, imitate and improve on them, dwell lovingly on any detail that lends itself to ornament. If he is a worker in iron and has to make some hinges and latch for a door that his neighbour is making for his cottage he will think of the door its shape and size and will see if he cannot make his hinges show up on the door, he will work an ornamental strap to cross the door, bind it together and give a look of strength and support. He will not want to make a hidden hinge that gives no explanation to the eye of how the door hangs and turns. All this will lead to the gradual beautifying of productions. William Morris, the great Poet-Craftsman, has told us that art is the expression of pleasure in work, and a man must have such conditions for his work as to be able to put art into it before he can enjoy it, the conditions in short of work done for a hobby!

Now I want to suggest tonight that we should aim at making all work hobby work. That instead of working a few hours a day at drudgery for a living and spending the rest in running a hobby, we should all be able to work at a hobby and live by our hobbies, that we should in short make our great aim to gladden the hours of labour rather than merely to shorten them.

4

The Art of Building a Home

*With Barry Parker. London, New York and Bombay,
Longmans, Green & Co., 1901.*

INTRODUCTION (WITH BARRY PARKER)

It is too often evident that people, instead of being assisted, and their lives added to, by the houses they occupy, are but living as well as may be in spite of them. The house, planned largely to meet supposed wants which never occur, and sacrificed to convention and custom, neither satisfies the real needs of its occupants nor expresses in any way their individuality.

The planning having been dictated by convention, all the details are worked out under the same influence. To each house is applied a certain amount of meaningless mechanical and superficial ornamentation according to some recognized standard. No use whatever is made of the decorative properties inherent in the construction and in the details necessary to the building.

. . . .

Could we but have the right thing put in the right place and left alone, each object having some vital reason for being where it is, and obviously revealing its function; could we but have that form given to everything which would best enable it to answer the real purpose for which it exists; our houses would become places of real interest.

. . . .

Let us call in the artist, bid him leave his easel pictures, and paint on our walls and over the chimney corner landscapes and scenes which shall bring light and life into the room; which shall speak of nature, purity, and truth; shall become part of the room, of the walls on which they are painted, and of the lives of us who live beside them;

47

paintings which our children shall grow up to love, and always connect with scenes of home with that vividness of a memory from
childhood which no time can efface. Then, if necessary, let the rest
of the walls go untouched in all the rich variety of colour and tone, of
light and shade, of the naked brickwork. Let the floor go uncarpeted
and the wood unpainted, that we may have time to think, and money
with which to educate our children to think also.

ART AND SIMPLICITY

Looking over some colour prints from Japan, I have been much
impressed by the extreme simplicity which characterizes the interiors
of Japanese houses as depicted in them. Print after print shows us a
room almost bare, the walls in some delicate brown or grey tint,
with the wood framing exposed: . . .

. . . .

How different is the common estimate of art and refinement here
in the west. When we think of the elaborately upholstered houses of
our 'artistic circles,' the people of taste—crowded as they are with
costly decorations and ornaments; . . . what wonder if philosophers
and moralists tell us that art is the enemy of simplicity, the fosterer of
luxury!

Knowing that the family will practically live in the kitchen, he
[the architect] would think out the space needed to give room for
doing work, taking meals, and resting (Fig. 14). He would consider
what of the work which must be done most tends to make the living-
room uncomfortable and dirty; and he would banish that to a scullery
or wash-house. In the living-room he would plan so that there might
be warm seats round the fire in winter, free from draughts, and seats
for summer near the window; a good dresser for work, well lighted
and supplied with cupboards, plate-rack, and perhaps a small
washing-up sink for the crockery. Then he would allow space for a
table for meals, and a few shelves for books; . . . Remembering too
that cleanliness has been placed only second among virtues, and that
probably most of the labourers would have dirty and arduous work,
he would contrive to give a bath; and if nothing better could be done
might put it in the scullery.

48

Perhaps the next commission is for a country house. It is stipulated that there shall be dining-room, drawing-room, and library, a good entrance hall and six bedrooms, together with kitchen, scullery, two servants' bedrooms, butler's pantry, china pantry, larder, laundry, a lavatory and cloak-room on the ground floor, and a bathroom on each bedroom floor. Such requirements have probably as little real connection with the lives of the people who are to live in the house, as the conventions which dictated the two roomed cottage.

.   .   .   .

Somewhere between those two extremes must lie the sort of house which the lover of art and beauty would desire for himself. Somewhere, in each case, must the two opposing tendencies of comfort and simplicity meet. Up to a certain point it will add to a man's real pleasure in life to enlarge upon the bare shelter of the labourer's cottage; but beyond that point any gain there may be, will be, too dearly bought. . . . It is sufficient for our purpose to realize that there is such a point, and that the development of a man's love of beauty and art will in the long run give more and more force to the tendencies which make for simplicity. . . . Working on these lines there will be a good chance that our homes will grow beautiful, that they will fit our lives, and be really filled with life.

OF FURNITURE

Just as in the middle ages the great hall was the centre of the house, all the other chambers clustering round and being subordinate to it; so in the modern middle class house a good living room is the first essential, and all the other rooms should be considered in relation to it (Fig. 8).

OF BUILDING AND NATURAL BEAUTY

But if we look for it, we shall find that modern suburbs specially offend in coming between the town and the country; so that, however the city may be fitted to beautify the landscape, we cannot see it from the fields; nor can we catch a refreshing glimpse of the cool green hillside from amidst our busy streets. For between lie miles of jerry cottages built in rows, or acres of ill-assorted villas, each set in a scrap of so-called landscape garden.

. . . .

Much of the charm of old buildings is no doubt due to the kindly hand of Time, which not only heals the scars that man makes on the earth, but tones down the raw surfaces, and softens the hard lines and colours of anything he may build. . . . If we take for example their position: do not old houses and villages generally seem to nestle in a valley, under a hill, or by the edge of a wood or copse, and both by their placing and style convey the idea of shelter and retreat? Sometimes this characteristic was carried so far, that we find houses placed

Fig. 8   Design for a living room with sanctum, kitchens, offices and bedroom around, from The Art of Building a Home, *1901. The centralizing, two story plan derives from the architects' admiration for the medieval great hall (cf. Fig. 40). It also signifies the appearance of their "gathering" instinct. At the right is a characteristic inglenook. The exposed brick, rough plaster, leaded glass, and mural also exemplify the vibrancy of their somewhat undisciplined early work during the Buxton period. Parker began as a mural painter and textile and wallpaper designer.*

so as to get little or no view. But they were built for busy people who lived mainly out of doors, and returned to their shelter at night as the rooks come home to roost. Too often now we place a building so as to strike a note of defiance with surrounding nature.

.   .   .   .

Then, too, does not the old building seem almost to grow out of the ground on which it stands? Built of the local stone; roofed with material common to the district—thatch, stone shingles, or grey slates, perhaps; harmonizing in colour with the rocks and soil; it is appropriate to the earth on which it rests, as the twig built nest of the rook is to the tree top on which it sways so lightly and yet so securely.

.   .   .   .

Many an old building that has little pretension to fine architecture, yet adorns a scene of natural beauty by its simple fitness of design, where a modern one would probably spoil it. Such design was the outcome of a natural effort to get the most use and convenience out of materials thoroughly known. Hence a general suitability is found between design and material, and an obvious connection between quaint features and the want that has called them into being. . . . In fact, we read in these old buildings, as in an open book, of a simple workman who was something of an artist, one who could take pleasure in this work, finding joy in the perfection of what he created, and delight in its comeliness.

CO-OPERATION IN BUILDING

The village was the expression of a small corporate life in which all the different units were personally in touch with each other, conscious of and frankly accepting their relations, and on the whole content with them. This relationship reveals itself in the feeling of order which the view induces. Every building honestly confesses just what it is, and so falls into its place. The smallest cottage has its share of the village street on to which the manor house also fronts (Fig. 25). It is content with that share and with its condition; and does not try to look like a villa. It is this crystallisation of the elements of the village in attendance with a definitely organized life of mutual relations,

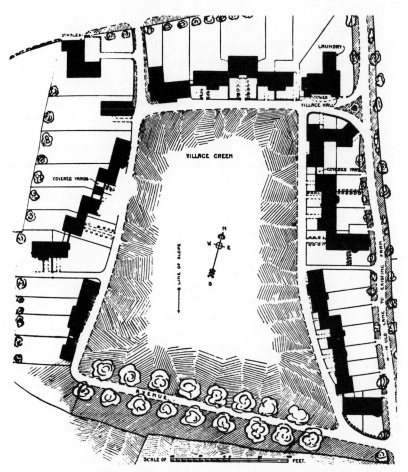

Fig. 9   Plan for a Hamlet, from The Art of Building a Home, *1901. This was
the earliest suggestion of a grouping of various combinations of houses and a break
in the building line. It was intended to give a unified impression from the standpoint
of a traditional village green (cf. Fig. 50), which was supposed to serve the same
communal gathering purpose out-of-doors that the two story living room did for the
family inside. The thought was to draw people to a place so that favorable and
positive things might begin to happen among them. This is probably the hamlet
scheme they exhibited at the Manchester Art Workers' Guild in 1903 and was related to their layout of New Earswick in 1902 for the Rowntree family near York.*

respect or service, which gives the appearance of being an organic whole, the home of a community, to what would otherwise be a mere conglomeration of buildings.

. . . .

The relationships of feudalism have gone, and democracy has yet to evolve some definite relationships of its own, which when they come will doubtless be as picturesque as the old forms. But allowing full force to these disadvantages, we could, if we really desired it, even now so arrange a new building site that it should not be an actual eyesore, and might manage that it should have some little of the charm of the old village.

. . . .

In all the large towns are numbers of people who hate the ugly and dreary life that they are condemned to live in them, who love the country and country life, and who will travel long distances to and from their work that they may be able to enjoy them. These people do not want to live in isolated houses, out of sight of their neighbors; they are townspeople of sociable instincts: but neither do they desire to live in a mere extension of the fringe of the town.

. . . .

The common insatiable desire for detachment is very remarkable; it appears to arise mainly from a resigned acceptance of the jerry builder's party wall as the inevitable one. Everyone suspects a party wall, looks to hear through it his neighbour's child in the dead of night, or his piano on a Sunday afternoon. Guarantee a soundproof party wall, and few will be able to give any valid reason why there should be from ten to fifty feet of useless ground between every two houses. In a properly built house, one is really much less conscious of one's neighbour, and much less over-looked by him, if his house is attached, than if it is a few yards away. Where it is desired, however, many minor devices, such as a highly walled garden or a covered-in yard, may be used with effect to increase the number of separate houses without destroying the grouping.

Artistically, the success of the plan would depend largely on the clustering of the buildings, the avoidance of mere rows on one hand and of detached villas on the other (Fig. 9). But, in addition, some controlling influence must maintain a certain degree of harmony. The use of local material as far as possible should be encouraged, and the introduction of discordant colours or styles of building be prevented. The extremist degree of simplicity should be allowed, but anything pretentious, showy, or false, be rigidly excluded.

. . . .

Society is, however, now realising very fast that this independence is no end in itself, and is only good in that it sets free the individuals to form new relationships based on mutual association.

5

Cottage Plans and Common Sense

(Fabian Tract No. 109) London, The Fabian Society, 1902.

How to provide for the Housing of the People is a problem for which our larger municipalities are now being compelled to find some solution; and all over the country these bodies are busy preparing plans for housing schemes. Social reformers are generally agreed that the people must be housed outside the congested town areas; many, like the Garden City Association, advocating the creation of entirely new towns. Such thoroughgoing schemes are hardly yet practicable for municipal bodies; but under the Housing Act of 1900 they now have power to build outside their own districts: and in the following remarks on the character of the houses required it is taken that the best policy for the municipalities is to build attractive cottages on the outskirts of their towns, always having due regard to the reasonable accessibility from these houses of places of employment and centres of interest and amusement.

. . . .

Modern building bye-laws have already done something towards securing air-space to every house, though, as will presently appear, there are methods of defeating their object, which they do not at present touch. But a sufficiency of air may be regarded as an acknowledged first condition for every decent house. The necessity for sunshine has still to receive the same public recognition; and there can be no doubt that our present knowledge of the importance of sunlight to health makes it needful to add to the first condition a second, that every house shall be open to a sufficiency of sunshine. Every house should at least get some sunshine into the room in which the family will live during the daytime.

. . . .

The essential thing is that every house should turn its face to the sun, whence come light, sweetness and health. The direction of roads and the fronting to street are details which must be made to fall in with this condition, or to give way to it.

By no means the least advantage which will arise from giving to aspect its due weight will be the consequent abolition of backs, back yards, back alleys and other such abominations, which have been too long screened by the insidious excuse of that wretched prefix *back*. For if every house is to face the sun, very often it must also have "its front behind"—as the Irishman expressed it. The little walled-in back yard is of course somewhat firmly established in the public affection: entrenched behind the feelings of pride and shame, it appeals alike to those who are too proud to be seen keeping their houses clean and tidy, and to those who are ashamed to have it seen how unclean and untidy they are. To encourage pride is a doubtful advantage, while it is a positive disadvantage to weaken in any way the incentive towards cleanliness which shame might bring. Like lumberrooms, too, these yards constitute a standing temptation to the accumulation of litter, far too strong for the average mortal to resist: old hampers, packing cases, broken furniture and such like find a resting-place there in which to rot, instead of being promptly disposed of. They are but wells of stagnant air, too often vitiated by decaying rubbish and drains. Back yards have, of course, their uses and advantages. They are convenient for the younger children to play in; but, alas! how very unsuitable! Too often sunless, always dreary, the typical back yard, shut in with walls and outbuildings, is about as sad a spot as one could offer to children for a playground. The coster may keep his barrow there, and the hawker sort his wares; while as open air washhouses something may be said for them. But some of these uses are occasional only, and too much must not be sacrificed for them, while the rest may be met in other ways. It does not seem to be realized that hundreds of thousands of working women spend the bulk of their lives with nothing better to look on than the ghastly prospect offered by these back yards, the squalid ugliness of which is unrelieved by a scrap of fresh green to speak of spring, or a fading leaf to tell of autumn.

. . . .

Some space to each house, however, there must be, even in towns. If, instead of being wasted in stuffy yards and dirty back streets, the space which is available for a number of houses were kept together, it would make quite a respectable square or garden. The cottages could then be grouped round such open spaces, forming quadrangles opening one into the other, with wide streets at intervals. Every house could be planned so that there should be a sunny aspect for the chief rooms, and a pleasant outlook both front and back. At present it is too often the custom to draw out a cottage plan that will come within a certain space and then repeat it unaltered in street after street, heedless of whether it faces north, south, east or west. Nothing more absurd or more regardless of the essential conditions could be imagined. Every house should be designed to suit its site and its aspect; and this is not less necessary when dealing with small houses built in rows, but more so.

There is something at once homely and dignified about a quad-rangle (Fig. 10) which gives it a charm even when the buildings are quite simple and unadorned. There is a sense of unity, of a complete whole, which lifts it out of the commonplace in a manner that nothing can accomplish for a mere street of cottages. Each square could have some individuality of treatment, the entrances could be utilized to produce some little central feature, and the effect of thus grouping small cottages to produce collectively a larger unit in the street, of a scale capable of assuming some dignity, would be such an improvement as will not readily be realized by any who have not seen what a few simple college quads may do for an otherwise com-monplace street. An Oxford or Cambridge college is simply a collec-tion of separate small tenements, built in squares, with some central common buildings. It is undoubtedly the most satisfactory arrange-ment for numbers of such tenements where the space is limited. In this manner from twenty to thirty houses, according to size, can be arranged to an acre, including streets; and this number should no-where be exceeded except under very great pressure. Even if it must be exceeded, probably it is better to go up and make extra floors, let in flats, than to curtail the open space. One larger space of ground is more effective than a number of small yards.

Squares, such as suggested, would always be sweet and fresh, being open to the sun and large enough to be airy without being draughty. The distance across, preventing the overlooking of windows, would ensure the essential privacy of the house, in spite of the want of back

Fig. 10 Quadrangle from Cottage Plans and Common Sense, *1902. The quad was another motif of Parker and Unwin and arose from several sources, including the colleges of Cambridge and Oxford, where Unwin was brought up (cf. Fig. 44). The ideal was again to promote association and then cooperation. The quad was also used during this first phase to accommodate the superblock deriving from model villages like Port Sunlight.*

yards. The space in the centre would allow a few trees to grow, some gardens to be made, and a safe play place for the children to be provided, while it would afford a pleasant and interesting outlook for all the cottages.

.   .   .   .

That a municipality could build living rooms at the top of an alley 24 ft. long, with windows only 11 ft. from the face of the opposite house, and could call that "clearing the slums" affords surely some measure of what slums must be. From such rooms the sun is effectually excluded, whatever their aspect; little fresh air will penetrate to the ends of those blind alleys; and a drearier outlook one would hardly have thought it possible to conceive. But, alas, it *has* been conceived; and on a fine estate near London there are to be found houses of this type having kitchens (sure to be used as living rooms) the windows of which look into alleys only 10 ft. 3 in. wide; these windows project, and the fronts are just 6 ft. 3 in. apart, while between them rise blackened wood fences exactly 3 ft. from each window! These houses are specially planned to accommodate two families, being provided with two living rooms and two outlets to the back. To realize how bad this type of house is, one has but to consider how they would appear in the light of the most lenient building bylaws if the doors from the main buildings to the projections were built up, making each house into two cottages technically, as already it is two virtually. Some municipalities would then consider themselves almost justified in pulling down such projecting cottages, to let air and light reach the others. They are virtually "back to back" houses opening on to 11 ft. wide streets with a dead end. Where houses must be built in rows, it is difficult to get enough air and sun to them in any case; and it is only possible to do this when all projections which can cause stagnation or shade are avoided. Every house in a row should contain all its rooms and offices under the main roof, and present an open and fair surface to sun and air on both its free sides. If so built it matters not which side is to the street, or which to the court; both are alike presentable; the aspect can govern the arrangements of the rooms unhampered by superstitions of front and back.

59

The self-contained house is not only better but more economical. A given cubic space can be built more cheaply when it is all within the main walls and under the main roof. A somewhat greater width of frontage is needed, and where streets are already laid out there might be extra cost of ground due to this which would be greater than the saving in the building. But the narrow house with straggling projections (Fig. 11A, B) requires greater depth; and the deeper the houses the greater is the expense of the side streets which has to be divided among them. Where land is to be laid out, if the quadrangle arrangement is adopted, there need be no waste in side streets, be-

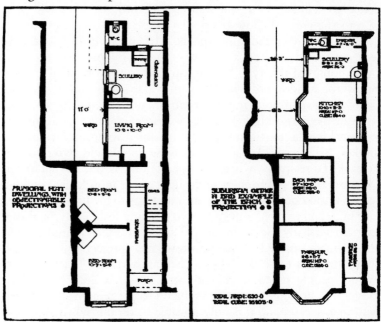

Fig. 11, A, B   Municipal house from London at left compared with a London suburban house from Cottage Plans and Common Sense, *1902. Unwin's contention was that the narrow street frontage forced a back projection and robbed the dwelling of air and sun, whether in city or suburb. This kind of late nineteenth-century palliative reform, when joined with the wide and straight bye-law reform street, he questioned. Like Morris, he felt half a loaf worse than none. As he expands the house and garden frontage, he thinks of ways of cutting the number and length of streets to compensate.*

cause the houses face all ways, and this would about balance the extra cost of street per house due to the wider frontage, while the saving of detached outbuildings and back yard walls would mean a considerable economy (Figs, 12, 13).

. . . .

This living room, then, will be the most thoroughly used and in all ways the chief room of the house; here the bulk of the domestic work will be done, meals will be prepared and eaten and children will play, while the whole family will often spend long evenings there together. The first consideration in planning any cottage should be to provide a sunny aspect and a cheerful outlook. In it there should be space to breathe freely, room to move freely, convenience for work, and comfort for rest. It must contain the cooking stove, some good cupboards, and a working dresser in a light and convenient place. No box of 11 or 12 feet square should be provided for this purpose.

. . . .

In planning the room the furniture should always be arranged and drawn in, to make sure that provision has been made for work and rest, for meals and play. Many a room is ruined because the dresser, the table, and the settle, have not been tried in on the plan.

Windows facing the street are much less depressing if slightly bayed to invite a peep up and down as well as across; a projection of a few inches in the centre, with some advantage of the thickness of the wall to set back the sides, will suffice to add very much to the outlook.

With regard to windows, doors, cupboards, and all other fittings, it should not be forgotten that when a quantity is required, as is usually the case in housing schemes, no extra cost is entailed by having them well designed, and of good proportions (Fig. 14). Money is often spent in bad ornament, which but detracts from the appearance of the buildings; but an elegant mould or shaping costs no more than a vulgar one, and a well proportioned door or mantle is as easily made as one ill-proportioned. That nothing can be spent on the ornamentation of artisans' cottages is no excuse whatever for their being ugly. Plain and simple they must be, but a plain and simple building well-designed may be very far from ugly.

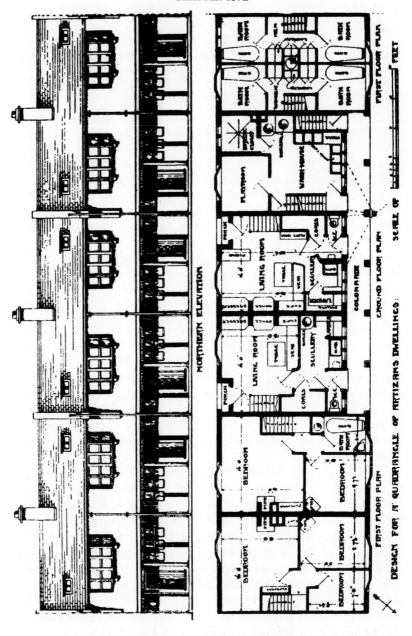

NORTHERN ELEVATION

FIRST FLOOR PLAN

GROUND FLOOR PLAN

FIRST FLOOR PLAN

DESIGN FOR A QUADRANGLE OF ARTIZANS DWELLINGS: SCALE OF FEET

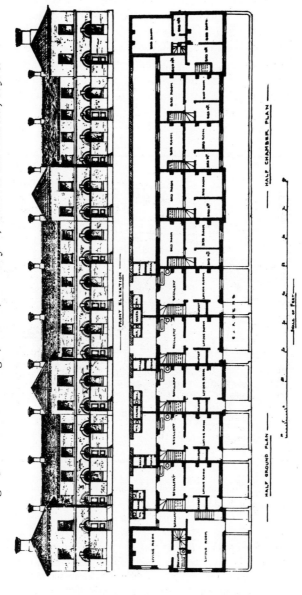

Fig. 12 Houses for a Quadrangle of Artisans' Dwellings, from Cottage Plans and Common Sense, 1902. The north side has an overhang for shelter from the rain. The comparison with model cottages of fifty years earlier at Saltaire (Fig. 13) shows a greater interest in well-proportioned, built-in furniture, inside coal closet and water closet and an upstairs bath, as well as a recommendation for communal baths, playrooms, and wash-houses. The stairwell was opened to the living room. The overhang, plaster, and mannered proportions date it about 1900.

Fig. 13 Workmen's Cottages, Saltaire, near Bradford, Lockwood and Mawson, 1850's.

Any one who has known what it is to occupy a large airy house-place will not readily sacrifice its advantages for either a needless parlor or a useless passage. For the question is not whether it is an advantage to have either a passage or parlor in addition to a decent living-room, but whether it is worth while to have either at the sacrifice of the living-room. A desire to imitate the middle-class house is at the bottom of the modern tendency to cut the cottage up into a series of minute compartments.

In small houses, such as we are considering, the 500 or so cubic feet

Fig. 14 Built-in range, working dresser and cupboard from the houses of Fig. 12. The aim was to face squarely the traditional working class usage of the living room for cooking and heating and to keep the furniture out of the middle. The few good books, a fireside seat, pictures, handmade strap hinges, were cultivated features to filter down to the working man, the good or better man, together with a better or-dering of his economically limited space. Sensitivity, responsibility, a warmth of familial feeling resulting from the refurnishing and reorganization of architectural or urban arrangements were now becoming leitmotifs.

of air space which are usually shut up in a staircase and landing, would be much more useful if thrown open to the living-room. That there is any advantage at all, either to that room or to the bedrooms, in having this "buffer state" of stagnant air between them, seems extremely doubtful; while there can be no doubt at all of the immense gain of having an extra 500 feet of air in a room which contains, perhaps, only 1,400 feet altogether, and many rooms contain less. The space should in any case have ventilation, and direct light is, of course, desirable. The extra height which would be obtained by throwing stairs and landing open to the living-room would greatly help in keeping that room well ventilated, as also would the possibility of having a window open so far from the occupied parts of the room.

. . . .

A bathroom for every cottage is an ideal which some day will surely come to be regarded as essential. In small tenements where the cost of this ideal may still be prohibitive, there seems no reason why there should not be provided at least a bathroom to each quadrangle (Fig. 12). One of the great advantages of substituting open courts for narrow streets would be the ease with which some little corporate feeling might be fostered in them. In municipal housing schemes, which spring from the co-operative effort of the whole town or city, it would seem specially fitting that something should be done to foster associated action among the tenants. And this is the more urgent because it is only by such association that we can hope to provide for the many some of the most desirable conveniences of life which wealth now enables the few to secure for themselves individually. We have already pointed out what advantage would arise from the associated use and enjoyment of the small plots of land which are all that can be given to each cottage. It has been found quite practicable in very many flat-dwellings to have a considerable amount of associated usage of wash-houses, sculleries, drying-grounds, etc., even among the most unenlightened tenants. There is no reason why the same arrangement should not be made with cottages. Quadrangles lend themselves peculiarly to the provision of small laundries, baths, reading-rooms, and other such simple and easily managed co-operative efforts.

A well-fitted wash-house having a plentiful supply of hot and cold water laid on to all the tubs, a proper washing and wringing machine, and a heated drying closet, is out of the reach of even the well-to-do cottager. But there is no reason why one or two such should not be provided for each court of houses; no reason why every little scullery should be blocked up with inadequate washing appliances; why every woman should have to spend a whole day toiling at the weekly wash which she could do with less labour in an hour or two if she had the use of proper apparatus; or why every living-room should be encumbered with clothes-horses or made uncomfortable with steam. The capital cost that would be saved by not providing space for, and fitting, washing appliances in all the sculleries, would pay for the one cooperative wash-house. And a very small addition to the rent would allow for the provision of hot water and heat for drying. To such a laundry should be attached a small room divided from it by a glazed screen, where little children could play under the mother's observation. The want of such a place prevents many a mother from using a public laundry, as also does the distance from home, and the necessity of conveying clothes to and fro through the public streets, objections which would not be present in the quadrangle with its small laundry. One or two baths, heated from the same source, could be provided; and it might be found possible to lay on a hot water supply to each cottage from the same centre. This has been done by the Liverpool Corporation in their Dryden-street houses, where a constant supply of hot water is provided to every sink at a charge of twopence per week to each tenement. This arrangement would greatly simplify the problem of providing baths to each house, as it would save the cost of the separate hot water installations. It is very desirable that a bath should have hot water attached, but one with cold water only is a great advance on none at all; and, in plans for artizans' houses, every alternative arrangement should be well considered, and every effort made to provide a bath of some sort. A bath-room adjacent to the scullery, or even a bath placed in the scullery, may sometimes be contrived when space on the bedroom floor is out of the question. And there are several alternative arrangements for getting a supply of hot water from the copper or side boiler direct into the bath. Where, however, a bath-room to each house is out of the question, one or two baths could easily be worked in connection with the laundry. Add to these a recreation or reading-room (also being tried at the Dryden-street houses) and there would be in each quadrangle a small co-operative centre, the attendance on which might easily be arranged to be undertaken by the tenant of the next cottage, for a small payment.

Such a centre would, by associated effort, provide for each cottager many advantages which he could not hope to secure for himself by his individual effort, and all for the payment of a few pence per week extra rent. Beginning with the laundry and baths, the most necessary and well-tried items, such cooperative centres would undoubtedly grow, as experience taught the tenants the advantage of association in domestic work; the common-room to supply somewhat the place of the individual parlor, the bakehouse, and even the common kitchen would be matters only of time and the growth of self-restraint, and the co-operative spirit. As the communal centre grows in importance, it will begin to affect our architecture, forming a striking feature in each court and giving a more complete sense of unity to it. At some point it may become worth while to have a covered way from the cottages to the common rooms—care being taken, of course, to put this only where it will not shade any sun from the house. But this is, perhaps, wandering too far into the future, leaving the immediately possible for the ideally desirable. Nonetheless, it is along these lines that we must look for any solution of the housing question in town suburbs which shall be satisfactory from the point of view of health and economy, and at the same time afford some opportunity for the gradual development of a simple dignity and beauty in the cottage, which assuredly is necessary, not only to the proper growth of the gentler and finer instincts of men, but to the producing of that indefinable something which makes the difference between a mere shelter and a home.

6

Town Planning in Practice:
An Introduction to the Art
of Designing Cities and Suburbs

London. T. Fisher Unwin, 1909

CHAPTER I. OF CIVIC ART AS
THE EXPRESSION OF CIVIC LIFE

THE last century has been remarkable, not only in this country but in some others, for an exceedingly rapid and extensive growth of towns. In England this growth has produced most serious results. For many years social reformers have been protesting against the evils which have arisen owing to this rapid and disorderly increase in the size of towns and their populations. Miles and miles of ground, which people not yet elderly can remember as open green fields, are now covered with dense masses of buildings packed together in rows along streets which have been laid out in a perfectly haphazard manner, without any consideration for the common interests of the people. It is not to any design adopted for the benefit of the whole that we are indebted for such semblance of order or convenience as may be found here and there in these new areas. The very complete system of country roads following usually the lines of old tracks, and made for convenience of access to and from the town, has undoubtedly formed a connecting frame for the network of streets which has sprung up along and between them. A part of these developments, too, has taken place on estates of large size, where there has been a limited possibility of comprehensive planning and where it has been to the advantage of the individual owner to consider the convenience of a tolerably large area. But for these two circumstances, the confusion of our town plans would have been even worse than it is. To-day it is hardly necessary to urge the desirability of a proper system of town planning. The advantage of the land around a growing town being laid out on a plan prepared with forethought and care to provide for the needs of the growing community seems self-evident; and yet it is only within the last few years that any general demand for such powers of town planning has been made. The corporations and other governing bodies have looked on help-lessly while estate after estate around their towns has been covered with buildings without any provision having been made for open spaces, school sites, or any other public needs. The owner's main interest, too often his only one, has been to produce the maximum increase of value or of ground rent possible for himself by crowding upon the land as much building as it would hold. The community, through its representative bodies, having watched the value of land forced up to its utmost limit, has been obliged to come in at this stage and purchase at these ruinous values such scraps of the land as may have been left, in order to satisfy in an indifferent manner important public needs. In this way huge sums of public money have been wasted.

In the year 1898 Mr. Ebenezer Howard published a little book entitled "To-morrow," in which all this was very forcibly stated, and in which he suggested that it would be comparatively easy to try the experiment of developing a town on the precisely opposite and obviously rational method of first making a plan, and, by the exercise of foresight, providing in that plan for all public needs likely to arise, and then securing the development of the town along the lines of this plan. This scheme was so obviously rational and desirable that in a comparatively short time it attracted the attention of a sufficient number of reformers to create a strong Garden City Association; and as a result of their efforts in popularising the idea, in the year 1903 an estate was purchased of about 3,800 acres at Letch-worth in Hertfordshire, by the First Garden City Company, upon which there has now come into being the nucleus of a considerable town.

This movement was too theoretical and experimental to appeal very widely to the English people, but another book was forth-coming of quite a different character. "The Example of Germany," by Mr. Horsfall, first published in 1904 (University Press, Manchester), showed how in Germany the same problem of rapid increase of towns had been dealt with on lines much akin to those advocated by Mr. Howard. Unfortunately, the English people do not in very large numbers read books in foreign languages; and until the publication of Mr. Horsfall's book turned general attention to the matter it was known to only a few in this country that for many years in Germany, and indeed in many other countries, orderly planning and designing of town development formed a part of the ordinary routine of municipal government. Since the publication of Mr. Horsfall's book the facts have become generally known. International congresses of housing reformers and architects, the exchange of international courtesies, between municipal bodies, and the work of various associations and individuals, have contributed to spread the knowledge that powers for planning and controlling the development of their cities more or less on the lines of those possessed by Germany are enjoyed and successfully used by the municipalities of most countries except America, France, and England up to the present time. This is the kind of evidence which the Englishman likes, and on the strength of this the demand for town planning powers has become so general and so influentially backed by municipal corporations that the Government has already passed through the House of Commons a Bill conferring upon municipalities some, at any rate, of the necessary powers; and it is confidently expected that such a Bill will become law during the present year.

Although we have only just realised the importance of the comprehensive and orderly planning of our towns, it must not be supposed that nothing has hitherto been done to cope with the evils raised by their rapid growth. On the contrary, much good work has been done. In the ample supply of pure water, in the drainage and removal of waste matter, in the paving, lighting, and cleansing of streets, and in many other such ways, probably our towns are served as well as, or even better than, those elsewhere. Moreover, by means of our much abused building bylaws, the worst excesses of overcrowding have been restrained; a certain minimum standard of airspace, light, and ventilation has been secured; while in the more modern parts of towns a fairly high degree of sanitation, of immunity from fire, and general stability of construction have been maintained, the importance of which can hardly be exaggerated. We have, indeed, in all these matters laid a good foundation and have secured many of the necessary elements for a healthy condition of life; and yet the remarkable fact remains that there are growing up around all our big towns vast districts, under these very bylaws, which for dreariness and sheer ugliness it is difficult to match anywhere, and compared with which many of the old unhealthy slums are, from the point of view of picturesqueness and beauty, infinitely more attractive.

The truth is that in this work we have neglected the amenities of life. We have forgotten that endless rows of brick boxes, looking out upon dreary streets and squalid backyards, are not really homes for people, and can never become such, however complete may be the drainage system, however pure the water supply, or however detailed the bylaws under which they are built. Important as all these provisions for man's material needs and sanitary existence are, they do not suffice. There is needed the vivifying touch of art which would give completeness and increase their value tenfold; there is needed just that imaginative treatment which could transform the whole.

Professor Lethaby has well said, "Art is the well-doing of what needs doing." We have in a certain niggardly way done what needed doing, but much that we have done has lacked the insight of imagination and the generosity of treatment which would have constituted the work well done; and it is from this well-doing that beauty springs. It is the lack of beauty, of the amenities of life, more than anything else which obliges us to admit that our work of town building in the past century has not been well done. Not even the poor can live by bread alone; and substantial as are the material boons which may be derived from such powers for the control of town development as we hope our municipalities will soon possess, the force which is behind this movement is derived far more from the desire for something beyond these boons, from the hope that through them something of beauty may be restored to town life. We shall, indeed, need to carry much further the good work begun by our building bylaws. We shall need to secure still more open ground, air-space, and sun-light for each dwelling; we shall need to

71

make proper provision for parks and playgrounds, to control our streets, to plan their direction, their width, and their character, so that they may in the best possible way minister to the convenience of the community. We shall need power to reserve suitable areas for factories, where they will have every convenience for their work and cause the minimum of nuisance to their neighbours. All these practical advantages, and much more, may be secured by the exercise of powers for town planning; but above all, we need to infuse the spirit of the artist into our work. The artist is not content with the least that will do; his desire is for the best, the utmost he can achieve. It is the small margin which makes all the difference between a thing scamped and a thing well done to which attention must be directed. From this margin of well-doing beauty will spring.

In desiring powers for town planning our town communities are seeking to be able to express their needs, their life, and their aspirations in the outward form of their towns, seeking, as it were, freedom to become the artists of their own cities, portraying on a gigantic canvas the expression of their life.

Beauty is an elusive quality, not easily defined, not always easily attained by direct effort, and yet it is a necessary element in all good work, the crowning and completing quality. It is not a quality that can be put on from outside, but springs from the spirit of the artist infused into the work. We are too much in the habit of regarding art as something added from without, some species of expensive trimming put on. Much of the restless, fussy vulgarity we see about us springs from this mistake. So long as art is regarded as a trimming, a species of crochet-work to be stitched in ever increasing quantities to the garments of life, it is vain to expect its true importance to be recognised. Civic art is too often understood to consist in filling our streets with marble fountains, dotting our squares with groups of statuary, twining our lamp-posts with wriggling acanthus leaves or dolphins' tails, and our buildings with meaningless bunches of fruit and flowers tied up with impossible stone ribbons. William Morris said: "Beauty, which is what is meant by Art, using the word in its widest sense, is, I contend, no mere accident of human life which people can take or leave as they choose, but a positive necessity of life, if we are to live as Nature meant us to—that is, unless we are content to be less than men." The art which he meant works from within outward; the beauty which he regarded as necessary to life is not a quality which can be plastered on the outside. Rather it results when life and the joy of life, working outwards, express themselves in the beauty and perfection of all the forms which are created for the satisfaction of their needs.

Such exuberance of life will, indeed, in due course find expression in the adornment of its creations with suitable decoration, and such adornment may become their crowning beauty; but the time for this is not yet. While the mass of the people live in hovels and slums and our children grow up far from the sight and pleasure of green fields and flowers; while our land is laid out solely to serve the interests of individual owners, without regard to the common needs, this is no time to think of the crowning beauty of ornament. We need to begin at the other end. Our immediate business is to lay a firm foundation.

Remembering then that art is expression and that civic art must be the expression of the life of the community, we cannot well have a more safe practical guide than Mr. Lethaby's saying that "Art is the well-doing of what needs doing." Does the town need a market-place, our rule would teach us to build the best, most convenient, and comely market-place we can design; not to erect a corrugated-iron shed for the market and spend what would have done this work well in "decorating" the town park with ornamental railings. First, let our markets be well built and our cottage areas well laid out; then there will soon grow up such a full civic life, such a joy and pride in the city as will seek expression in adornment. This is not the place to consider in detail the many causes which have led to the rapid growth of town populations. The concentration of industry, the decay of agriculture, the growing contrast in the conditions of life offered in the country and the town, have all had their influence in leading people in such vast numbers to forsake the lonely cottage on the hillside or the sleeping village in the hollow in favour of the dirty street in the town slum. The impulse partly springs from the desire for higher wages and the attraction of varied amusement and flaring gas lamps; but it equally arises from the desire for a greater knowledge, wider experience, and fuller life generally which men realise they can only find in closer association with their fellows. But whatever their motives in leaving their villages, the people have broken many old ties of interest and attachment; it should be our aim to secure that in going to the city they may find new ties, new interests, new hopes, and that general atmosphere which will create for them new homes and new local patriotism. Hitherto our modern towns have been too much mere aggregations of people; but it must be our work to transform these same aggregations into consciously organised communities, finding in their towns and cities new homes in the true sense, enjoying that fuller life which comes from more intimate intercourse, and finding in the organisation of their town scope and stimulus for the practice and development of the more noble aims which have contributed to bring them together.

Aristotle defined a city as a place where men live a common life for a noble end. The movement towards town improvement of which town planning forms but one branch must have for its aim the creation of such a city as shall at once express the common life and stimulate its inhabitants in their pursuit of the noble end. With the expression of the common life, as we have already seen, town planning is intimately concerned, and whether our cities will indeed become great works of art will principally depend on the prevalence of the aim towards a noble end to which Aristotle referred. It is, indeed, from this expression that civic art must draws its inspiration and guidance. We are told by many authorities that expression is one of the fundamental elements in all art, and that the creation of great art results when some great idea is finely rendered. It is probable that in the art of city building great work will again be done when there is a fine common life seeking expression, and when we have so mastered the technique of our art as to have established a tradition capable of giving adequate form to such expression.

Before attempting to consider in detail the various practical problems of town planning, it will be useful if we can understand something of the reasons which exist for the general lack of beauty in our towns, and further if we try to arrive at some principles to guide us in determining in individual cases what treatment is likely to lead to a beautiful result and what to the reverse. We have become so used to living among surroundings in which beauty has little or no place

74

that we do not realise what a remarkable and unique feature the ugliness of modern life is. We are apt to forget that this ugliness may be said to belong almost exclusively to the period covered by the industrial development of the last century. We do not find evidence of it before that period, in our own towns or in those of a character to be compared with our own in other countries. It is not that in other respects older towns excelled modern ones; it is not that they were less overcrowded, that their streets were finer, better kept, or cleaner. On the contrary, excessive overcrowding existed in old towns; the streets were usually very narrow, and at many periods were both dirty and insanitary. Nor does there appear to have been generally very much conscious planning of the streets. Often there is little apparent order or arrangement in the placing of the buildings; and yet, in spite of this, a high degree of beauty almost always marked the effect produced. So much so, that both in this country and in many others wherever one finds a street or part of a street dating from before what may be called the modern period, one is almost sure to see something pleasing and beautiful in its effect. The result, no doubt, is due largely to a greater degree of beauty in the individual buildings; many of these, in fact most of them, were quite simple and unadorned, yet there seems to have been such an all-pervading instinct or tradition guiding the builders in past times, that most of what they did contained elements of beauty and produced picturesque street pictures. Something also is due to the hand of time, which, through the sagging of timbers, has softened the lines of the buildings, and through the weathering of the surfaces has mellowed the textures of the materials used in them (Fig. 15). The influence of the tradition we have mentioned was not confined to the buildings themselves, but seems to have extended to the treatment of streets and *places* as well as to such minor details as steps, entrance gates, walls, and fences, which often enhance the beauty of the picture. To a very great degree this tradition appears to have acted unconsciously and almost as a natural force; for the absence of symmetry or orderly arrangement is often as evident as the picturesqueness of the architectural grouping is pleasing. In these old towns and streets we read as in an open book the story of a life governed by impulses very different from our own; we read of gradual growth, of the free play of

75

imaginative thought, devoted without stint to each individual building; while the simplicity of treatment, the absence of decoration or
ornament in the majority of cases, and the general use and skilled
handling of the materials most readily accessible, tell of the usual
avoidance of what could be called extravagance. Nevertheless, we
are impressed by the generous use of material and labour revealed
in the dimensions of the beams, in the thickness of the walls, and in
the treatment of all necessary features, which suggests that two
prominent elements in the tradition which influenced builders in old
times were that the work should be well done, and that it should be
comely to look upon when finished. While obviously the cost was
carefully considered, it was not deemed legitimate to sacrifice proper

*Fig. 15 Rothenburg, looking toward the Markusturm on the inner ring of the
early smaller town, from* Town Planning in Practice, *1909. Rothenburg was
the favorite European medieval town of Parker and Unwin, together with Nurem-
burg. It was the piling up and concentration of buildings within the limits of walls
and the picturesqueness of the streets which intrigued them. The influence is best
recorded in Hampstead Garden Suburb.*

76

construction, good design, or good finish in order to attain the last possible degree of cheapness. How different is the spirit in which the modern suburb is built up! A similar absence of planning or conscious design in the laying out, and an almost equal freedom to the individual builder to do as he likes mark the modern method; but with what a different result! There is little thought bestowed on the individual building, or on its adaptation to the site and surroundings, no imaginative fitting of it into a picture. Instead, some stock plan of a house which is thought to be economical is reproduced in row after row without regard to levels, aspect, or anything but just the one point, can the building be done so cheaply that it can be made to yield a good return on the outlay? Is it any wonder, then, that our towns and our suburbs express by their ugliness the passion for individual gain which so largely dominates their creation? How, then, it may be asked, are we to make any progress, for the passing of a Town Planning Bill will not change the character of the life which we see expressing itself in our dreary suburbs? And, indeed, if this desire for individual gain represented the only impulse of the citizens, it is little that we could hope to do. But happily this is not the case. There is much that is great and splendidly co-operative in the life of our towns, and our social instinct is already highly developed by the mutual helpfulness of common life. Therefore, though town planning powers will not change the individualistic impulses which prevail, they will for the first time make possible an adequate expression of such corporate life as exists. Here, as elsewhere, action and reaction will take place; the more adequate expression of corporate life in the outward forms of the town will both stimulate and give fresh scope to the co-operative spirit from which it has sprung.

The conscious art of town building is practically a new one for us in England. We shall need to begin somewhat tentatively, and at first we may well be content if we can introduce order to replace the present chaos, if we can do something to restrain the devastating tendency of personal interests and to satisfy in a straightforward and orderly manner the obvious requirements of the community.

Though the study of old towns and their buildings is most useful, nay, is almost essential to any due appreciation of the subject, we must not forget that we cannot, even if we would, reproduce the conditions under which they were created; the fine and all-pervading tradition is gone, and it will take generations for any new tradition comparable to the old one to grow up. While, therefore, we study and admire, it does not follow that we can copy; for we must consider what is likely to lead to the best results under modern conditions, what is and what is not attainable with the means at our disposal.

The informal beauty which resulted from the natural and apparently unconscious growth of the medieval town may command our highest admiration, but we may feel that it arose from conditions of life which no longer exist, and that it is unwise to seek to reproduce it. Possibly other forms of beauty will be found more adapted to our present conditions. The very rapidity of the growth of modern towns demands special treatment. The wholesale character of their extension almost precludes the possibility of our attaining that appearance of natural growth which we have admired in the medieval town, where additions were made so gradually that each house was adapted to its place, and assimilated into the whole before the next was added. We already see in the modern suburb too much evidence of what is likely to result from any haphazard system of development. Modern conditions require, undoubtedly, that the new districts of our towns should be built to a definite plan. They must lose the unconscious and accidental character and come under the rules of conscious and ordered design. We find that in the few instances in which towns were laid out as a whole in ancient times the plans usually follow very simple rectangular lines, and are quite different in character from those which developed by slow, natural growth. A short examination of the different types of town plans will perhaps be the most helpful way of approaching our subject.

CHAPTER II. OF THE INDIVIDUALITY OF TOWNS

. . . .

In America the tradition of a formal lay-out, usually on a rigid gridiron or checker-board pattern, has hitherto been little disturbed by any other style. Towns once started on this pattern have continued to grow to an enormous extent, until vast areas are covered by this regular, monotonous latticework of streets laid out in parallel lines, cutting up the building areas into rectangular blocks of equal size. The inconvenience and monotony of this arrangement are, however, now compelling the Americans to consider new systems. Diagonal streets are being arranged, and in some cases cut through the existing blocks, so that it will not be necessary on so many occasions to travel two sides of a triangle in order to go from point to point. The Americans, like ourselves, have hitherto been without municipal town planning powers, but the work of town improvement has been taken in hand by Commissioners, well supported, and much good work is being done under the guidance of able men like Mr. Mulford Robinson and Mr. Day. Special attention is being devoted to the provision of parks to break up the monotony of the towns and provide breathing spaces, also to the arrangement of wide boulevards and strips of parkway to link up the parks and so provide walks and drives about the town, passing through belts of park or garden.

The town of Philadelphia may be taken as illustrating many others. A plan of the town as designed by William Penn is given, the central square of which, marked "A," became the site of the City Hall, while four other squares or parks are shown. This plan seems in the main to have been followed, and the city has to a large extent grown on the rectangular lines thus laid down, as will be seen by reference to the plan of the modern town, where the City Hall and the Logan and Franklin Squares will enable the portion included in Penn's design to be identified (Fig. 16). The regularity of the plan has been in various parts broken by tracks which had been established before the growth of the town reached these points, but has tended to reassert itself after passing these roads. Numerous straight, diagonal roads and parkways are now being planned, and one of these, leading from the City Hall to the Fairmount Park, passing diagonally across Logan Square, is shown as at present marked on the city plan. A complete design for the treatment of this parkway and the Logan Square, prepared for the Fairmount Park Art Association by Horace Trumbauer, C. C. Zantziger, and Paul P. Cret, is also given (Fig. 17). In this plan the French treatment of developing along vistas

79

Fig. 16   Plan of Philadelphia with the city hall marked A, as on Penn's plan, and
with diagonal avenues introduced, especially toward Fairmount Park at the left,
from Town Planning in Practice, 1909. Unwin's assumption was that America
held a certain stake in the checkerboard pattern and that Philadelphia was historic
proof of it. He took exception, however, to its monotony when developed beyond
Penn's original plan and observed that the railway lines and longer avenues were
modifying it.

with terminal features has been taken as a model, and numerous subsidiary vistas around the Fairmount Parkway have been planned. An imaginary bird's-eye sketch of this parkway at the Fairmount end will explain the proposal. Another illustration shows a further scheme which is under consideration for the treatment of League Island Park and the surrounding district, and the introduction of radial symmetrical diagonals into the gridiron of the street plan. The modern German school of town planners point out with much truth that this arrangement of diagonals crossing a square trellis system of streets, leaves numerous acute-angled plots which do not lend themselves to the production either of very successful groups of buildings or very useful open spaces. Too often a regular system of streets, once started, is continued quite regardless of the contours of the ground, and not only entails vast expense in levelling, but destroys any interesting character that may spring from a more perfect adaptation of the town plan to the conditions of the site. It will be interesting to compare with the plan of Philadelphia that of Washington, where the design includes a considerable number of diagonals.

In spite of the lack of municipal town planning powers, the civic spirit would appear to be strong enough in many American cities to carry out very extensive and costly improvements, and the numerous careful and exhaustive reports on city developments which are constantly being issued by voluntary associations, architectural societies, &c., are proof that the Americans are seriously taking in hand the beautifying of their towns. . . .

The geometrical system adopted by Baron Haussmann in his reconstructions in Paris was practised also by the Germans previous to 1889; but since the publication in that year of Camillo Sitte's book, "Der Städtebau," the French translation of which, under the title of "L'Art de bâtir les Villes," was published in 1902, there has been a marked change in the character of German town planning.

Camillo Sitte, by a careful study of plans of medieval towns, came to the conclusion that these were designed on lines which not only provided completely for the convenience of traffic, but were in accordance with the artistic principles upon which the beauty of towns must depend.

Impressed by the picturesque and beautiful results which sprang

Fig. 17 Fairmount Parkway in Philadelphia, by Trumbauer, Zantziger and Cret, from Town Planning in Practice, *1909. The art museum is on an acropolis at the end. Unwin was interested in the parkway, which he correctly identifies here as in the French style, because of its capacity to avoid going around the triangle of half a city block in its point to point movement. Unlike New York or Chicago with their skyscrapers, Philadelphia seemed more amenable and cultivatable to him. He is inclined to speak favorably about it and Washington, D. C., with its Lincoln Memorial, because the city beautiful movement was congenial to his own desire for urban beauty.*

from devious lines and varying widths of streets, and from irregular *places* planned with roads entering them at odd angles, the Germans are now seeking to reproduce these, and to consciously design along the same irregular lines. It is, indeed, maintained by Sitte and others that much of the irregularity characteristic of the medieval town which we have been apt to consider the result of natural and unconsidered growth was, on the contrary, deliberately planned by the ancients in accordance with artistic principles then well understood. Be this as it may, there can be little doubt that the true artistic tradition in the Middle Ages was so steadily maintained and so widely prevalent as to constitute almost an instinct in the people, which would lead them in dealing with irregularities arising from natural growth to do just the right thing in each case. The difference between this instinct which made the best of irregularities, and the conscious artistic designing of these irregularities, may seem a small one, but it is of importance when upon it is based the claim that the conscious designing of the modern town planner should be carried out on the same irregular lines.

If, for example, a modern German town plan such as that for Kufstein (Fig. 18), or the prize plan for the town of Pforzheim (Fig. 19), be compared with the plans of medieval towns such as Rothenburg (Fig. 20) or Bruges, it will at once be apparent how closely the modern school in that country are basing their work upon medieval models.

If, further, these same plans be compared with earlier work, such as may be seen in Cologne (Fig. 21), Antwerp, Düsseldorf, and many other towns, it will be equally evident how entirely the character of their work has changed since those plans were made, so much so as to constitute a complete change of style, a change as complete as in the field of architecture would be a Gothic revival following upon a period of Renaissance work.

The examples illustrated will give some idea of town planning as practised in Germany, and it is particularly evident from them how the earlier geometrical and more regular planning has given place to much more carefully considered but altogether irregular systems. The contrast is seen in the two examples of a portion of Stuttgart as planned in 1860 to 1870, and as finally revised in 1902. Several inter-

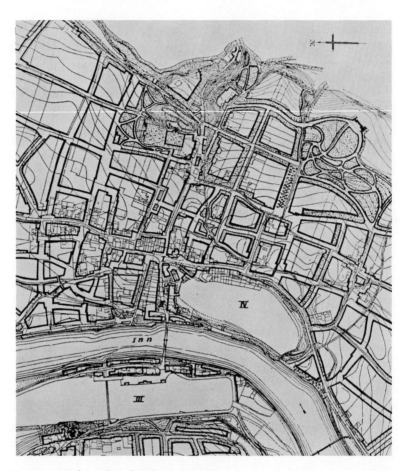

Fig. 18   Modern Plan of Kufstein, Germany, by Otto Lasne, from Town Planning in Practice, *1909. Kufstein and Pforzheim were for Unwin diverse examples of the informal layout adopted by the contemporary German planners after the publication of Sitte's book in 1889. How to distinguish between a slowly cumulative medieval tradition and a nineteenth-century speed and urgency was a question he often asked himself. He also noticed that each planner tended to execute his own personal style within this picturesque idiom. Lasne's was directed toward street pictures and closed vistas.*

mediate plans were made for this rather difficult area, each showing a more marked development of irregularity and adaptation to the contours than the one preceding it. It is noticeable also that considerable individuality of style distinguishes the work of different men. If the plans for Zschertnitz, for example, are contrasted with the sweeping lines which mark the plan of Grünstadt, and this again is compared with Flensburg, this variety will be evident; while the plan of Kufstein, with its very carefully worked out building lines designed to produce picturesque street pictures and closed vistas, shows perhaps better than any other the extent to which the modern

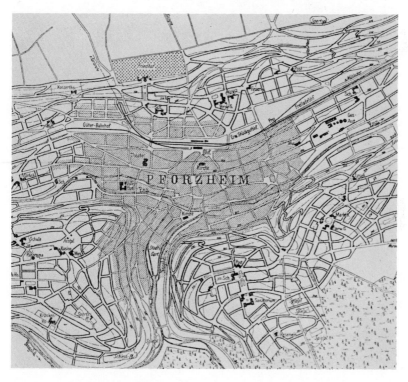

Fig. 19 Prize Plan of Pforzheim, Germany, by Thomas Langenberger, from Town Planning in Practice, *1909.*

Fig. 20   Map of Rothenburg in the year 1884, from Town Planning in Practice.

German School of town planners are trying to embody in their present work suggestions which they derive from their older towns. The three illustrations from Cologne serve to show the thoroughness of their work. The plans are worked out with increasing detail, and very large scale drawings of the streets and junctions are prepared before the work is executed. Some plans are specially prepared to show the division of the areas into plots, others to indicate the intended arrangement of planting, the treatment of open spaces, or the distribution of different classes of buildings. The Cologne examples may perhaps be classed as representing the period of transition from the geometrical to the modern systems.

The plans of Nuremberg are of special interest, showing one of the most beautiful German cities which has of recent years grown rapidly, and for which a town plan was completed as recently as 1907, covering a large area on all sides of the town. A portion of this plan is illustrated, and shows how the design has been adapted to the sporadic development which had already taken place on the area covered. However much we individually may like or dislike the particular style and the detail treatment adopted by the Germans, we cannot but feel the highest admiration for the skill and the thoroughness displayed in their town planning work; no labour seems too much for them, no number of revisions too great to be made so that they may bring their plans up to date and in accordance with the best style that is known and approved by the skilled town planners of their country; and, while there is much in their work that one would not wish to see copied in English towns, there can be no question as to the immense benefit to be derived from a careful study of that which has been accomplished in a field where they have been working earnestly for many years and where we are in comparison mere beginners.

While, however, the importance of most of the principles which Camillo Sitte deduced from his study of medieval towns may be as great as the modern German school thinks, it does seem to me that they are in danger of regarding these principles as the only ones of great importance; nor do they appear to realise how far it is possible to comply with these principles in designs based upon more regular lines. Some of the irregularity in their work appears to be introduced

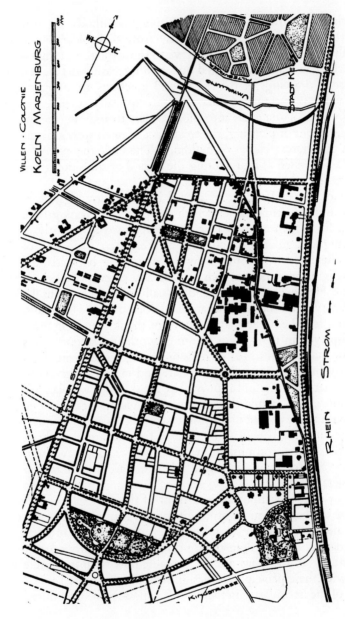

VILLEN · COLONIE
KOELN MARJENBURG

Fig. 21   Cologne Town Plan showing old line of fortifications and one of the southern suburbs, from Town Planning in Practice, 1909. This was used by Unwin to contrast the old-fashioned, pre-Sitte, French character of German town planning with Kufstein and Pforzheim (Figs. 18, 19). The contour adaption and medieval irregularity came after this more "geometric" system.

for its own sake, and if not aimlessly, at least without adequate reason; the result being that many of their more recent plans lack any sense of framework or largeness of design at all in scale with the area dealt with.

If we examine the plan of Rothenburg (Fig. 20), we see how, especially in the original old town, the scale of the principal *places* and streets is sufficiently large for them to dominate the town, and to provide for it a frame and centre points which render the whole really simple and easily comprehensible to the stranger, but in any such plan as that of Pforzheim (Fig. 19) one feels the same simplicity is lacking. In the case of towns arranged on land having such complicated contours as characterise the neighbourhood of Pforzheim, it is, of course, impossible to criticise the plan fairly without an intimate knowledge of the ground. The system of roads appears to be most admirably adapted to the contours; nevertheless this kind of plan, which is characteristic of much modern German work, seems lacking in the simplicity of framework and order of design which are needful to enable the plan of the town to be readily grasped. It would be very easy for a stranger to get lost in such a town. The same remarks apply to the town of Grünstadt, which covers a far smaller area. The continual repetition of small, irregular *places* and road junctions suggests a degree of artificial imitation of accidentally produced features hardly likely to lead to successful results in the hands of modern builders, who have completely lost touch with the tradition which apparently proved so successful a guide to our forefathers.

One point of great interest in the description which we have quoted of Sir Christopher Wren's plan of London may well be again mentioned here, namely, his proposal that the boundaries of all existing properties should be disregarded, and that the individual parcels of land should all be temporarily given into the hands of public trustees or commissioners so that they might be rearranged and the area divided, each person receiving back, not his own plot exactly, but as nearly as possible the equivalent of it in the shape of a plot of land arranged to suit the new roads and new groupings of buildings proposed. It is interesting to find thus early suggested by Wren a form of solution for this difficult problem in connection with town planning which has been adopted in Germany. The city of Frankfort possesses compulsory powers for thus rearranging boundaries of plots under what is known as the *lex Adickes*. Other cities have to depend on promoting voluntary arrangements for the exercise of indirect pressure to secure this rearrangement of plots. Where land is held in small lots, some such power of rearranging boundaries seems necessary for good planning to be possible; but there is much discussion among town planners in Germany on this point. Camillo Sitte and those who follow him argue that the necessity chiefly arose owing to the particular geometrical type of planning which was in vogue previous to his day, and that a freer type of planning, in which greater consideration could be shown for the existing conditions of the site for existing roadways and property boundaries, would render needless very much of the rearrangement of properties which the geometrical school of town planning found so necessary. It is further argued that the consideration of these existing conditions would lead to a type of plan having in it something of the interest and variety which characterise the towns of the Middle Ages.

.   .   .   .

CHAPTER VI. OF CENTRES AND ENCLOSED PLACES
.   .   .   .

The effect of enclosure in a *place* is so important that many methods have been suggested for obtaining some considerable degree of enclosure, even with the modern wide streets. In some cases the *place* may be formed entirely on one or both sides of a main thoroughfare having no outlets in the recessed portion of the *place* other than those of quite minor size, such as footways; and where there exists anything of a market in the old-fashioned sense, or where public buildings, such as the town hall, which numerous people must frequent, can be so situated as to keep the *place* well used, such a plan would be in many ways a good one; if the stream of traffic does not pass through it, there is always a danger that some other point will become the natural centre and the *place* itself become deserted and deteriorate in character.

Furthermore there are ways of securing a sufficient background for the buildings and a sense of enclosure in a fairly large *place* if the roads are so arranged that from the main points where people would stand to view groups of public buildings, they do not afford direct vistas. The roads may pass out of the square at right angles to the line of vision, or if along the line of vision, their direction may be diverted sufficiently early for the vista to be closed with other groups of buildings. In this way it may be possible to make a *place* in the traffic centre where it will be most constantly used, without sacrificing the frame and background required for the public buildings. Also it may be arranged that these same public buildings form terminal features along some of the main roads converging towards the centre of the town.

Enclosure, however, is not the only desirable effect to be produced. Professor Lethaby has pointed out in one of his lectures how carefully the view of the sea has been guarded in Constantinople. The views out of a town into the country beyond have always a special charm, and it may be well worth while to secure these distant views of sea and mountain, and even to bring into the heart of the town glimpses of sunset glory, where openings to the west can be secured.

One finds very charming little pictures at times at the ends of such long vistas. There is one from the Square at Lisieux. Indeed, these long vistas seem to have a special charm for the French people as they are commonly to be found in French towns. They are nonetheless pleasing to the eye because their effect cannot be conveyed in a photograph, where, as a rule, the distant vista fades away into vagueness. In like manner the return view along these open roads may be so arranged as to give those approaching the town a distant glimpse of its public buildings.

One simple form of *place* may be made at the junction of four streets by breaking the line of direction, the result being that the view down each street is closed and a figure resembling a turbine is produced; or the roads may be brought in at the corners of the *place* in such a way that, while giving plenty of space for the turning of traffic, the buildings will close the view.

The new market at Vienna (Fig. 22D) affords an example of the way in which the streets can be brought into a modern *place* without unduly breaking the frame of the buildings; while (Fig. 22 A, B, and

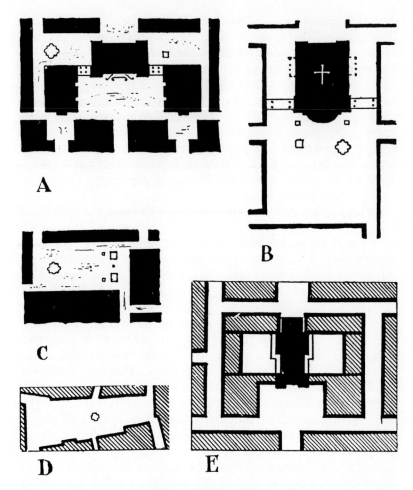

Fig. 22, A, B, C, D, E   Places *and groups of* places *adapted to modern conditions, as recommended by Camillo Sitte. D is the Neuemarkt, Vienna, not by
Sitte. From* Town Planning in Practice, *1909.*

E), taken from Camillo Sitte's book, show how these principles may be applied in regularly shaped *places* and groups of *places*. In each of these examples it will be noticed how *places* are formed to afford views of the different sides of the chief buildings and how the picture is made to develop itself in the main on concave lines. It is an important point to remember that, owing to the nature of vision, a group of buildings taking generally a concave line is likely to be more pleasing than one taking the convex line; and that where (Fig. 22B), the building must for some reason stand detached, projecting forward into the main *place*, it is a matter of great importance to link it up by means of arcades, or in some other way, so as to give it a frame and connection with the other buildings.

There is another type of *place* which is more of the nature of a forecourt to a building. The Piazza in front of St. Peter's in Rome is a well-known example; and in the laying out of Vienna, a *place* on somewhat similar lines was arranged in front of one of the churches, an illustration of which is given.

There is a fine group of regular *places* at Nancy, . . . In some parts a general sense of enclosure is secured, in others it is somewhat markedly wanting, although the elaborate iron gates and arcades which fill some of the open sides and corners go some way towards completing the picture, and are helped by the background of foliage.

Camillo Sitte was very emphatic in his opinion that the centres of *places* should be kept free from statues and monuments, and that these should be placed at the sides or in the corners, as in the Roman Forum or in the Forum of Pompeii. Many charming pictures of old street fountains and drinking troughs might be given showing how these will fall into the picture when not too much isolated. When statues are in the middle of busy roads they cannot be seen with comfort or safety and their effect is lost in the traffic.

Here, again, no definite rule can be laid down; there occur central points which one feels instinctively need to be marked and emphasised, and there occur other spaces where it seems of equal importance to avoid anything that would break up the simplicity of the space itself.

The plan of the town square at Letchworth (Fig. 23A) may perhaps serve to illustrate some of these points, though it was planned before

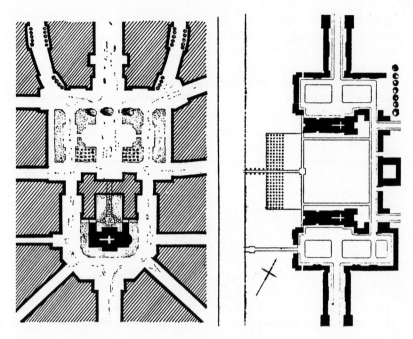

Fig. 23, A, B Letchworth Town Square at left; Hampstead Garden Suburb, Central Place on right, from Town Planning in Practice, 1909. Both communities were by Parker and Unwin, although Unwin states that he did Letchworth before he had heard of Sitte and Hampstead Square was actually arranged by Edwin Lutyens. The municipal buildings at Letchworth were not built as shown, nor was the church. Both squares tend to be more open and English than the Sitte schemes because there is a wish to look out and down over the landscape and also to emphasize internal voids. Unwin was anxious to avoid being rigidly formalistic on the one hand, or romantically capricious on the other.

the writer had the good fortune to come across Camillo Sitte's book. Here it will be seen that the square is the centre into which many roads converge from different parts of the town; and along several of these roads, particularly those to the east and west, views of the distant country will permanently remain open. A wide main avenue leads from the station to the Town Square and commands directly a view of the façade of the Municipal Buildings, these being the most important buildings dominating the square. It is intended that the roads on each side of them shall be partially closed by an arcade, while in any case they extend but a short distance before they diverge, and groups of buildings will close the vista and form a background for the Municipal Buildings themselves. The façades of the buildings on each side will also be in full view, up to the point where we see instead the ends of the square, so that a fair sense of enclosure in these two corners will be obtained. The roads branching off east and west from the front of the Municipal Buildings are placed at such an angle that a perspective view of the buildings will be obtained along them. The curves of Eastcheap and Westcheap will have somewhat the same effect in giving background and frame to the buildings on the north side of the square. On the south side of the Municipal Buildings it was intended to place the central church of the town, and views of this building were secured from east, west, and south, also from south-west and south-east, the south facade of the church being intended to be the main one; while the church itself was intended to form the south side of a smaller quadrangle of which the Municipal Buildings would form the other three sides.

With roads 40 or 50 feet wide, or even wider, as main roads in a modern town must usually be, unless the *place* is of considerable extent, it is very difficult to secure much sense of enclosure, particularly when, as in the instance just referred to, it is to be made in any sense a centre to the framework of roads, and all that will be possible in some cases will be to secure closed and completed street pictures from each of the roads leading into the *place*, or to secure definite sense of enclosure at one end or in certain corners.

The treatment of the central *place* in the Hampstead Garden Suburb (Fig. 23 B) may perhaps be taken as affording a contrast to that at Letchworth just described. Here the arrangement is on four-square

95

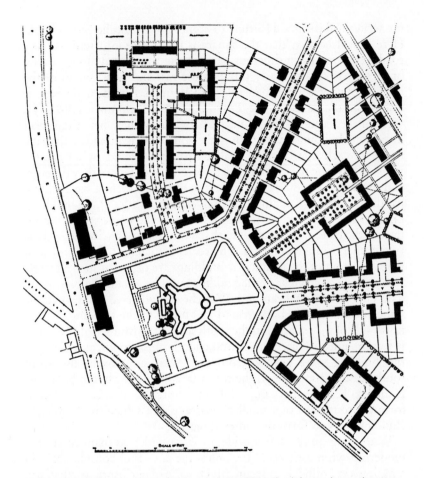

Fig. 24   Subsidiary center at Hampstead Garden Suburb by Parker and Unwin,
from Town Planning in Practice, *1909. All the streets fed down the slope to the
square which was protected from the road by two large clusters of shops. This section of Hampstead shows Unwin's planning at its best, and one sees quickly and
clearly within it his cul-de-sac device combined with the quadrangle, while taking
full advantage of the superblock, first brought out at Port Sunlight. The irregularity of the building line and the sense of villagelike order and containment would go
back to the hamlet of almost a decade before (Fig. 9). The inner spaces for playing
fields, like the cul-de-sacs and quads, were to foster neighborly association.*

lines, to suit Mr. Lutyens's fine Renaissance design for the whole of the buildings round this group of *places*. The two main approaches from the south and from the north lead up to enclosed *places*, the view being terminated by the north and south sides, respectively, of the church and the chapel. Between these two *places* is laid out a large open space or green, the western side being kept quite open, and the slope in the foreground planted as an orchard; while on the east a row of buildings with an institute in the centre overlooks this green. It is proposed to attach the vicarage, halls, and Sunday schools to the church and chapel to complete to some extent the enclosure on three sides of this larger *place*. The whole is situated on the flat top of rising ground, and the treatment has been adopted in order to combine a sense of enclosure in the *places* with a sense of space and openness in the green; and while securing background and frame to the main views of the chief buildings, to secure something of the wide outlook over the surrounding country which the rising ground affords. Particularly has the view of Hampstead Heath been kept open, and the view from it up into the central square. The roads entering from the east side lead up to the east end of the church, which will form the terminal feature of the street picture here also.

A subsidiary centre in the Hampstead Suburb (Fig. 24) has been formed by means of an irregularly shaped green, round which some of the smaller public buildings will be grouped.

Other examples of small subsidiary centres are afforded by the plans of the Ealing Tenants' Estate and that of the Anchor Tenants at Leicester. In the former case a wide avenue is made to serve as the central feature; one or two public buildings are arranged at points where the cross roads lead into this, and the avenue is laid out in such a way as to afford space for seats and wide, shady promenades.

In the latter case a small square is arranged as the centre, and here it is intended to build the institute, school, place of worship, and co-operative store, which are likely to be required by the community. In this scheme the necessity, for drainage purposes, of arranging one of the roads to follow pretty closely the contour lines of the undulating surface has been taken advantage of to bring two of the roads into the square diagonally, so that the views along them may be closed by the side of the square opposite them.

In the plan of Earswick, near York, a green, large enough to serve as a playing field and recreation ground, was taken as the most fit central feature for the village, and where the main road runs alongside of this green it is intended to arrange for a few shops, and for the grouping of the public buildings.

It is by no means easy to secure the proper development of centres; where an estate or district develops slowly there will always be some tendency for those interested in the various semi-public buildings, such as places of worship, shops, &cc., to take short-sighted views of the future development, and to insist on placing these buildings on sites adjacent to the first groups of houses built, so that it may easily happen that only to a limited extent can the centre be developed in the way originally intended. Nevertheless, it is well that the centre should be fixed and form the main feature of the plan. It is probable that in the full development of the scheme other public buildings whose requirement was not foreseen may help to fill up the centre, and as the public become somewhat accustomed to the use of foresight in the laying out of towns and suburbs, they will the more readily come to acquiesce in the placing of their public buildings on these pre-arranged central spaces.

CHAPTER VIII. OF SITE PLANNING AND RESIDENTIAL ROADS

. . . .

Both in town and site planning it is important to prevent the complete separation of different classes of people which is such a feature of the English modern town. Mrs. Barnett in her writings has laid special emphasis on this point and has referred to the many evils which result from large areas being inhabited entirely by people of one limited class. Indeed, it was one of her special aims in promoting the Hampstead Garden Suburb Trust to show to how much greater extent the intermingling of the different classes might be brought about. It is not within the power of the town planner to alter the prejudices of people, or to prevent entirely the growing up of the East End and West End in a town; but a good deal may be done in this direction by care and forethought; certainly within limits, more or less wide, there is no difficulty in mingling houses of different sizes. There is nothing whatever in the prejudices of people to justify the covering of large areas with houses of exactly the same size and type. The growing up of suburbs occupied solely by any individual class is bad, socially, economically, and aesthetically. It is due to the wholesale and thoughtless character of town development, and is quite foreign to the traditions of our country; it results very often in bad municipal government and unfair distribution of the burdens of local taxation, misunderstanding and want of trust between different classes of people, and in the development and exaggeration of differences of habit and thought; it leads, too, to a dreary monotony of effect, which is almost as depressing as it is ugly. In the English village we find all classes of houses mingled along the village street or around the green, from the smallest labourer's cottage to the large house of the wealthy farmer, doctor, or local manufacturer, and even at times there is included the mansion of the lord of the manor. How much this adds to the charm of the village street may be gathered from the illustrations given. If, then, the site that is being planned is one which we expect mainly to have a working-class population, we should still try to arrange some attractive corner in which a few rather larger houses may be built (Fig. 25); we should induce the doctor to live among his patients by affording him a suitable site, and give an opportunity for those who have been successful in life, and may have a little leisure to devote to the public work of the district, to live in suitable homes among others not so fortunate. And whether or not we shall succeed will depend very much upon the arrangement. We shall not, for example, expect to let plots for larger houses if the approach is arranged along a street of the smallest type of cottages.

In arranging our site plan we must keep in mind economy in the length and gradient of the roads, facility for drainage, and such practical matters. Where a road can be made to run at the bottom of a hollow, the arrangement will be found economical and satisfactory in many ways; the houses on each side being on ground slightly above the road, a minimum depth of drain will be required; while any surplus material arising from the excavation can usually be spread upon the road without raising it above the level of the houses. Roads

Fig. 25 Village Street, Kersey, Suffolk, from Town Planning in Practice,
*1909. The older English village was often cited by Parker and Unwin as offering a
lesson for living together among rich and poor, professional and tradesman, so this
is a visible emblem of the social and economic interdependence of a sympathetic
community life, with its large and small houses. This view also exemplifies the
street employed in an aesthetic rather than a purely utilitarian manner, a down
slope toward the open countryside, a plastic flow of space, which he particularly
tried to capture with Parker at Letchworth, and a rather restrained alternation of
stucco and half timber which could be contrasted with Norman Shaw's more
eclectic street pictures of a generation earlier, which had overcome monotony but
seemed to later urban designers to be too patchy or broken. It was during this time
that Unwin became especially aware of planes and three-dimensional forms as they
qualified spaces. This is a distinct and British version of the street pictures of
Cézanne and Utrillo in its cubistic or abstract undertones.*

following the lines of natural drainage are, therefore, from these practical points of view desirable, and difficulties of dealing with surface water will likely be avoided; where, on the other hand, roads run across hollows, they are likely to need filling and cutting, excessive depth of drain, excessive depth of foundations for the buildings where they face the banked portions of the road, and considerable expense for retaining walls and steps where the buildings face the cuttings. Where roads run along the hillside, it is usual to cut one side and fill the other, and this is probably the most economical arrangement from the point of view of the road itself; but it is wise to do more cutting than filling, and even more economical on roads intended for residences, particularly if the removal of the surplus material is easily manageable. In roads on the side of a hill the sewer must be laid deep enough to drain the houses on the low side; this adds considerably to the expense, while the plots on the low side are of less value because either the house will stand below the level of the road, which is not usually thought desirable; or it must be raised at considerable expense of extra foundation; it would therefore be wise to err on the side of cutting such roads to greater depth than would be done if the first cost of the road were alone considered.

The sites which stand above the road gain in attractiveness, except in the cases of large houses where a carriage drive is required, so that the cost of a retaining wall is not resented by the plot-holder in the same way that he is apt to resent the cost of extra foundations.

The question of the character of building roads in this country certainly requires much re-consideration. There are two circumstances which have complicated the situation. First, the width of roads has been used, under our form of building bye-laws, to determine the distance between the houses, and as a means of securing a greater degree of open space than would otherwise be obtained. The result is that the widths of roads under the bye-laws commonly in force in the English towns, are not regulated with regard to requirements of traffic, a minimum width for streets is arbitrarily fixed, 40 to 50 feet being usual, and all roads are required to be laid out at least this width; usually there is no power for the local authority to require greater width, although 40 to 50 feet is as utterly inadequate for the main roads of a town as it is excessive for the purpose of giving access to a few cottages. As a consequence, roads have to be widened at vast expense to allow for trams and for traffic, while cottages are built fronting to dreary wastes of asphalte and macadam, one half of which could with great advantage be added to their gardens or laid out as grass margin.

The second condition which greatly influences the character of our roads is that the cost of their construction is borne by the owners or lessees of the land and frontages, while the cost of maintenance, after they have become public roads, is borne by the local authority. The result of this is that in order to reduce as much as possible the liability of the public for maintenance, all roads are required to be finished in the most expensive and durable manner, irrespective of whether the traffic on them is likely to require or justify such expense. It is, of course, right and proper that roads should be sufficiently substantially made to carry their probable traffic, with a reasonable cost for upkeep; but the fact that the capital outlay is stipulated for by the party that pays for the upkeep and does not pay the first cost, has resulted in a very great waste of capital on roads where such outlay is neither justified by the requirements nor necessary to bring the upkeep within reasonable limits. A large residential hotel, a mansion such as Chatsworth or Blenheim, will be adequately served by a simple carriage drive from 13 to 20 feet wide. The population of such a building will be larger than that of a row or group of cottages and the amount of wheel traffic to and from it many times as great; yet for the cottage road asphalte or concrete paved footpaths, granite kerbs and channel, and granite macadamised surface, the whole from 40 to 50 ft. wide, and costing, with the sewers, &c., from £5 to £8 a lineal yard, are required by the local authority, under our existing bye-laws. It will be seen at once how this excessive cost tends to limit the frontage of the houses. Where an attempt is being made to build cottages under £200 in cost, the charge of £3 per yard for the half-share of the road becomes a serious matter, and the houses must suffer, both in size and frontage, to quite an unnecessary extent. Where traffic is likely to be heavy, and where the building roads will serve also to link up main roads or be likely in the future to develop into main roads, suitable provision must, of course, be made. But where, as frequently happens, it is virtually certain that the road will only be used for the daily visits of the milkman's cart and the daily rounds of the coal merchant's van or the doctor's gig, it is clear that a well-made track, more of the nature of a gentleman's carriage drive, with a grass margin on each side, and in some cases a simple gravel or paved footway of narrow width, for use in wet weather, is all that need be demanded; and that with the small amount of traffic coming down such a road, the maintenance against wear and tear would be no greater than in the case of the vastly more costly road usually required.

The cost of roads varies very much, according to the price of material and labour in the district, and according to the requirements of the local authorities. In some cases a separate system of drainage is provided for surface water, which of course adds heavily to the cost, though it is probably a most desirable arrangement from the point of view of sewage treatment. The authorities in some districts permit the sewers to be laid in the roads at depths as shallow as will allow for the reasonable drainage of the houses to be built. In other districts greater minimum depths are required to provide against future contingencies, and to protect the pipes from possible injuries, owing to the passage of traction engines and other heavy traffic. In some districts drains are allowed to be laid in the ground without concrete; in others a bed of concrete under the drains is required, while in some places drains need to be entirely surrounded by concrete. These and many other such details affect the cost of roads so that it is not possible to give any estimate. Further, it must always be remembered that the cost of a road may mean one of two things—either the construction of the road in accordance with the bye-laws for the purposes of building, or this, plus the cost of making up the road to suit the standard of perfection which will be expected when the road is taken over by the local authorities. The owners or lessees of the plots fronting to the road are legally liable for this latter expense. It is usual for the landowner who lets out the site to bear the first cost, but custom varies considerably as to how much of the work is included in the first cost and how much in the second. Sometimes the road is so thoroughly made up to begin with that the subsequent cost is reduced to a minimum. At other times the preliminary making up of the road is only carried to such an extent as will give an effective cartage road for building operations; and the kerb and channel are laid, and any paving and asphalting to the footpaths carried out after the road is built up, and when it is about to be taken over by the local authorities. Where building operations are being carried out on an extensive scale by the same person or body who is responsible for the making of the roads, probably it is better to be content with the simple building road in the first instance, and to make up the road properly once and for all when the buildings are completed, and it is about to be taken over; it is often found when a road has been pretty thoroughly made in the first instance and some time elapses before it is taken over, that it is so damaged by the building operations—kerbs and channels chipped and displaced, and the surface so deeply scored with ruts—that the local authorities practically re-make the surface, re-lay kerbs and channels, &c., before they will accept the road, which entails a very heavy cost. In some districts, however, building operations are not allowed to be commenced until the road is made and the kerb and channel laid, and in these cases there appears to be no option to the builder in the matter. The whole question of the apportionment of the costs of construction and maintenance of roads and their character seems to need thorough investigation, and it is to be hoped that the interest in such matters roused by the town planning movement will result in this being done.

To meet this difficulty to some extent the Hampstead Garden Suburb Trust obtained an Act of Parliament (the main clauses of which are given in "Practical Housing" by J. S. Nettlefold), under which the width of road to be constructed according to bye-laws was limited to 40 feet, and the Trust were allowed if they made their roads of greater width than 40 feet, to devote the extra space to grass margins in which trees could be planted. At the time the Act was passed the local bye-laws fixed 40 feet as the minimum width for all roads, but new bye-laws were being prepared in which 50 feet was fixed as the minimum. Another clause allowed the Trust to construct roads not exceeding 500 feet in length of a width of 30 feet, provided that the houses on each side of such roads should not be nearer to one another than 50 feet. By the same Act, on the other hand, the Trust agreed to limit the number of houses to the acre, on the average over the whole of the estate, to 8. This Act suggests that the local authorities might offer an inducement to landowners, and others developing estates, to limit the number of houses to the acre by offering concessions in the matter of road construction. Reference to the Hampstead Suburb plan will show that these short roads have been extensively used and have led to the formation of many groups of houses around greens, tennis-courts, and squares which could not practicably have been arranged without the powers given under this Act. It will be seen from the Act that it is not intended that these roads should be taken over by the local authorities, and although 20 feet is dedicated for the purpose of the road, in many cases a carriage drive of 13 or 14 feet is all that it is intended to construct. Many of the main roads in the suburb will exceed the minimum of 40 feet, some being 50 feet and some 60 feet, and in these cases usually grass margins planted with trees will be provided. Special concessions have also been made with regard to the character of the roads on the estate of the Harborne tenants in Birmingham. In other cases—as, for example, in the village of Earswick, near York, and at the Garden City at Letchworth —no bye-laws as to the character of roads and streets have been in force, and it has there been possible to experiment with roads of various characters and widths. . . .

The direction of the building roads must be considered from every point of view, besides that of drainage and convenience of construction. The question of the aspect of the buildings is an important one, and here the site planner is often in the difficulty of being obliged to lay out the roads without knowing, or having any control over, the character of the buildings which will be placed upon them. In such cases there is no doubt that roads having their direction mainly north and south have a very great advantage in that the houses will have a fair amount of sunshine on both their open sides. Where roads run east and west the houses will get more sun on the south side, but, on the other hand, the north sides will get but little in the summer and none in the winter. Many people desire a south front to their house, and roads having a general direction east and west are desirable from this point of view, if the buildings can be arranged and planned accordingly. Houses with a south aspect need a greater frontage, as all the best rooms should be on the south side, and in the case of houses on the south side of the road which have a north aspect, there is, especially with small houses and cottages, the difficulty that the front of the house should be to the garden. Without very careful planning this is liable to result in untidy backs to the road, but with care may result in a most attractive type of house, having its best rooms overlooking the garden and away from the dust and noise of the street. It is probably best, on the whole, that the roads should not be cut quite due east and west, so that either in the early morning or in the late afternoon during the greater part of the year the sun may shine on the more northerly side of the buildings. The relative advantages of a southern outlook and of an east and west outlook will vary according to the latitude of the house. Taking the latitude of London, it will be seen that for the few winter months the advantage of the south front is very great, but that for the remainder of the year an east and west aspect secures a very large amount of sunshine on both sides of the house, and has the advantage of giving sunny and shady rooms for both morning and afternoon, and avoiding the excessive heat of the midday sun.

. . . .

While, therefore, taking the whole year round, there can be no doubt that an aspect south or slightly west of south may be considered the most desirable for dwelling rooms, it will be found that where dwelling rooms must be placed on both sides of the house, ample sunshine would be secured with an east and west aspect through the greater part of the year, and that during the summer months a considerable amount of sunshine would penetrate windows facing somewhat north of east or west.

Table showing relative Duration in Hours per Annum of actual Sunshine before and after Noon recorded at four Stations, the Average for fifteen Years being taken.

	Valencia.	Aberdeen.	Falmouth.	Kew.
Before noon	700.46	655.88	840.87	700.23
After noon	758.55	682.66	895.02	760.64

In France, where a road runs north and south and it is desired to give the houses a southern frontage, one often sees little rows of houses placed with their ends to the road, access being obtained by a simple pathway. It would seem desirable to modify the usual form of building bye-laws to allow of this arrangement, under certain restrictions as to the number of houses and as to the distance apart of the rows. We shall refer to the matter of aspect again in dealing with the setting out of the building plots; meantime another consideration must be borne in mind, namely, that of the wind. It is certainly not desirable to have too many roads following unbroken for any considerable distance the line of the prevailing winds, or of those winds which are likely to be violent or to produce excessive dust. Here, again, local conditions must be borne in mind, though, speaking generally for this country, south-west is probably the prevailing direction of the wind.

. . . .

In undulating or hilly countries the question of the gradients of the roads will very largely influence their direction. On a main traffic road a gradient greater than 1 in 30 may be regarded as a disadvantage, though for short distances steeper gradients may not be a serious drawback, and building roads with steeper gradients may be used where sufficient reason exists. In some districts the special charm of the site may be its elevation, and it may be desirable to emphasise this by carrying certain roads and ways straight up the hillside, with little or no regard to the steepness of the gradient. Undoubtedly one finds in old towns many beautiful examples of such steep streets, as at Clovelly in our own country, and at Dinan in France.

The steep street, however, adds very greatly to the difficulties of building, and although the clever handling of problems due to these difficulties may lead to very beautiful and picturesque results, there is no doubt that the common methods of dealing with buildings on steep sites by means of a number of repeated steps or jumps in the roof, or still worse by means of the sloping line of roof which is carried parallel to the road instead of being kept square with the floor line, are so unsatisfactory that it would be prudent to avoid aiming at the special effects to be derived from steepness, unless one is fairly sure that the designing of the buildings will fall into capable hands. In places where small subsidiary roads can be used—and one must hope that all places may soon be included in this category—it may even be wise where a main road runs through a building estate to arrange the houses so that most of them front on to such subsidiary drives, only a few having a frontage direct to the main road. The character of modern traffic, particularly the present character of motor traffic, has rendered frontage to the main road anything but desirable for residence; the dust, the noise, the smell are all objectionable features; and though at first sight it may seem extravagant not to make use of the main frontage it would not be found so in practice, the subsidiary roads costing comparatively little. Moreover, it is not possible to utilise the whole of the frontage both on the main and the cross roads to the utmost extent, and if the frontage on the smaller side roads is more desirable, little will be lost by sacrificing a portion of the main road frontage.

With reference to the desirability of straight or curved roads little need be added to what has already been said with regard to the main roads of the town, except that in the planning of sites for residential purposes greater freedom of treatment may well be adopted, the stateliness which may be desirable for the treatment of the central portions of the town not being appropriate very often to the residential district. The width apart of the buildings on residential sites will tend to give greater freedom in the treatment of the street pictures; and where the streets are planted with trees and the houses set back considerably from the road, a good deal of freedom may be taken in the treatment of the two sides; but whatever the character of the street, it is of the utmost importance to avoid mere aimless wiggles.

7

Nothing Gained by Overcrowding!
How the Garden City type
of development may benefit
both owner and occupier

London, Garden Cities and Town Planning Association, 1912.

. . . .

THE fact that many of these [presently existing] towns have already far exceeded the limit of size which is deemed desirable by the advocates of the Garden City is, no doubt, unfortunate, but it can hardly be urged as a good reason for making no protest from the Garden City point of view against these towns being allowed to continue to grow in a homogeneous manner, swallowing up and obliterating the country all round, like the spreading of flood water over a shallow valley. Nor is it enough that the Garden City movement should urge that suburban development be carried out with such a relation between the amount of building and open space as would accord with the detailed principles advocated for a Garden City. If it is deemed desirable to limit the size of a new town like Letchworth to something like 35,000 people and to plan for an agricultural belt to intervene between this town and the federated townlets which may be permitted to spring up around it, surely it is still more desirable to make some effort to secure definite belts of open space around existing towns and to encourage their development by means of detached suburbs grouped around some centre and separated from the existing town by at least sufficient open ground to provide for fresh air, recreation and contact with growing nature.

This federal aspect, if we may so term it, of town development has the great advantage of expressing in outward form the natural organisation of a large community.

People tend to flock together in villages or towns that they may enjoy the advantages of social intercourse with the wider opportunities for pleasure and culture that spring from it, and that they may enjoy the material advantages which arise from the co-operation of many individuals working for some common purpose. But it is impossible to secure effective action from any large number of people if they all try to act directly. Effective individual co-operation is limited to the comparatively small number who can have immediate personal knowledge of each other and can come into immediate and constant personal relation. Such a limited number of individuals form a group, and where other similar groups exist they cannot effectively co-operate as individuals, but each group must as a whole come into contact with another group through the medium of some central person representing the group. In the same way when the number of minor groups results in the selection of so many representatives that they exceed the number possible for individual co-operation, these representatives must again form a larger district group and come into contact with others through some district representative. This is what we mean by organisation, and though it takes many different forms the essential features are common to all the forms, whether to the companies and regiments of an army, acting through and controlled by their officers, the lodges or districts of a friendly society, or the departments and work shops of a great industry.

This basic principle of organisation should find its expression in the form of the town which, instead of being a huge aggregation of units ever spreading further and further away from the original centre and losing all touch with that centre, should consist of a federation of groups constantly clustering around new subsidiary centres, each group limited to a size that can effectively keep in touch with and be controlled from the subsidiary centre, and through that centre have connection with the original and main centre of the federated area.

In the development of existing towns therefore, the Garden City principle has much to offer which is of the greatest value because it is based on the natural principles of organisation and would give expression in outward form to such organisation. Detaching the units or suburbs one from another, giving them each their subsidiary centre around which they should be grouped, and upon which they would depend, while the overgrown centre might have to remain a larger unit than is desirable, it would yet be possible to secure limitation to the units constituting the new growth and to secure between these units and between them and the parent town some defining and dividing belt of open land which would be of inestimable value.

.   .   .   .

But, as in the larger field the Garden City movement defines the proper relation and proportion between urban and rural and between residential, industrial and recreational areas, so within these areas it defines in detail the relation and proportion between the buildings themselves and the ground surrounding them; and it is this aspect of the question I wish chiefly to consider, for it will be found that much the same economic principles which determine the possibility of limiting the proportion of the individual building to the surrounding garden space, will also influence the limitation of the proportion of urban area to surrounding country.

The overcrowding of buildings upon the land has been so generally practiced, and is so generally assumed to be necessary, that one cannot hope to advance far without first considering carefully whether there is any economic difficulty standing in the way of limiting the number of houses or other buildings to be erected upon a given area of land, and if so, what that difficulty is.

To most people, whether they are interested in the land as owners or builders, or are disinterested inquirers, it seems at first sight so obvious that the more houses you put upon each acre of land, the more economical is the use made of that land, and the less will each person have to pay for it, that few have really troubled to test the matter. It has generally been assumed that though it may be necessary, to some extent, to put a limit to the number of houses that may be crowded upon an acre, that this limit should be made as high as possible, and that any limitation must necessarily be a serious tax upon the community.

111

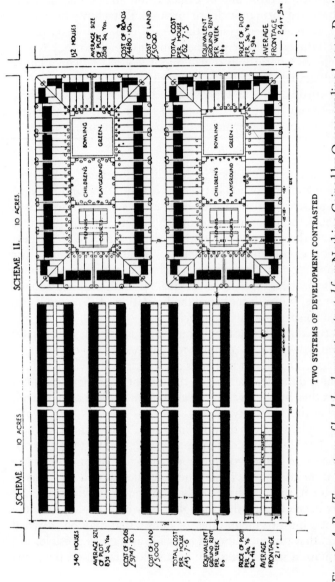

TWO SYSTEMS OF DEVELOPMENT CONTRASTED

Fig. 26, A, B   Two systems of land development contrasted from Nothing Gained by Overcrowding!, 1912. Despite the large number of interdependent figures, the principles involved between schemes I and II are comparatively simple. The first is a progression from the old bylaw street to the superblock. The second is that by reducing the number and length of streets, developmental costs could be cut and more inner green space provided. Both of these forms really came from the North of England, and represent the conflict and drama of that area more than London.

112

It can, however, be shown that this view is very far from correct; that on the contrary, the greater the number of houses crowded upon the land, the higher the rate which each occupier must pay for every yard of it which his plot contains, the smaller will be the total return to the owners of land in increment value, and, indeed, the less will be the real economy in the use of the land.

I do not say that nobody can obtain advantage from overcrowding buildings; that point we will deal with later, but first let us, by definite figures, thoroughly establish the facts. This can best be done by taking two exactly similar areas of ground and working out the costs of development with the larger and smaller number of houses to the acre.

As a first example we will take the conditions as they exist in many large towns, where bylaws of the usual type are in force, and where provision is made for a back road to give access to the cottage yards, and we will assume two schemes of development for similar areas, each containing ten acres of land, measured to the centre line of the surrounding road.

Fig. 26A shows one of these ten acres developed with approximately the maximum number of houses permitted under modern improved bylaws, assuming the type of house which occupies 16 feet of frontage. It will be seen that a total of 340 houses can be placed upon the ten acres, at the rate of thirty-four houses to the acre, the roads being included in the measurement. These houses are built up to the road line; the roads are made 42 feet wide, and back passages are provided 9 feet in width.

Fig. 26B is developed in accordance with the Garden City principles. The houses are to be of the same size and occupy the same frontage as before; but instead of being built in continuous rows they are built in groups of two, four, or six, and a space is left between each group; in addition to this, provision is made for passageways through the groups so that direct access is obtainable to all the gardens from the front roads, and no back roads are required. In this case only 152 houses are arranged for on the ten acres, that is at the rate of 15.2 houses per acre, considerably less than half the number of houses in Fig. 26A.

In both cases the value of the land before development is assumed to be £500 per acre, the main roads to cost £7 5s., and back roads £1 per lineal yard. These costs of course include not only the making of the roads and the laying of the drains, but also the making up of the roads when they are taken over by the Local Authorities, as both these costs have, in one form or another, to be borne by the cottage. Although very often the owner or builder may incur the first cost, and he may leave the purchaser of each plot to bear the second, it is necessary, for fair comparison, to take the total cost of the road.

The following table gives the cost of development in each case, that is, the main costs of land and road making, together with the average size and cost of plot and the equivalent ground rent on a 4 per cent. basis. Some of these figures are also given at the side of each scheme in Fig. 26.

Table 1

	Scheme I With land at £500 per acre.			Scheme II With land at £500 per acre.			Scheme II With land at £250 per acre.		
Number of houses	340			152			152		
Average size of plot	83½ sq.yds.			261½ sq.yds.			261½ sq.yds.		
Cost of roads	£9,747	10	0	£4,480	10	0	£4,480	10	0
Cost of land	£5,000	0	0	£5,000	0	0	£2,500	0	0
Total cost of land and roads per house	£43	7	6	£62	7	5	£45	18	6
Equivalent ground rent per week		8d.			11¾d.			8½d.	
Price of plot per sq. yard	10/4½			4/9¼			3/6		

It is apparent that in Fig. 26A a large proportion of the ground must be occupied by the roads, to provide frontage for the large number of houses. In Fig. 26B the greater part of this land is available to be added to the gardens, or to be arranged as recreation grounds in addition to the gardens, as shown in the diagram. Now roadways represent perhaps the most expensive form in which open space can be provided: not only so, but every additional road means a serious loss of frontage available for building, because at every point where one road joins another there is lost not only the frontage occupied by the width of that roadway but the frontage occupied by the depth of the building and plot. In Fig. 26A it will be seen that the whole of the frontage of the vertical roads is occupied in this way, and is therefore ineffective for the purpose of affording frontage for buildings. There is, of course, a similar loss at each corner in Fig. 26B, but there are only eight corners where the loss can occur, while there are twenty such corners in Fig. 26A. Thus it happens that the greater the number of houses crowded upon an area of land, the greater must be the length of road provided per house, the greater the proportion of the land occupied by roads, or, in other words, the greater the waste of the land. It will be seen from the table how this affects the area of the plot and the cost of the roads. In Fig. 26A there are only 83½ square yards of ground actually available for the building and backyard, while in Fig. 26B an average of 261½ square yards is available. Although the number of houses has only been reduced by rather more than half, the area of the plot has been increased more than three times.

The cost of the roads in Fig. 26A comes out at £9,747 10s., while in Fig. 26B in spite of the much more liberal provision of frontage, to allow for passages between every pair of houses and spaces between every group, it only comes to £4,480 10s. The cost of the land in each case would be £5,000. If this is added to the cost of the roads in each scheme, and that total divided by the number of houses arranged for, it will be found that in Fig. 26A the cost of the small plot of 83½ square yards is £43 7s. 6d., equivalent to a ground rent of 8d. a week on a 4 per cent. basis, while in Fig. 26B the cost of the large plot of 261½ square yards has only risen to £62 7s. 5d., equivalent to a ground rent of 11¾d. per week. From the point of view of the tenant, therefore, in Fig. 26A, he pays £43 7s. 6d. for the freehold of 83½ square yards of land, equivalent to a price of 10s. 4½d. per square yard. In Fig. 26B he pays £62 7s. 5d. for the freehold of 261½ square yards, which is at the rate of 4s. 9¼d. per square yard.

Let me ask whether in purchasing any other commodity, the public are content to take such very bad value for their money. Supposing there were two village shops, and one offered to supply eighty-three common marbles for 8d., and the other one offered 261 marbles of the same size and character for 11¾d., can it be supposed that there would be any village boy who would not know which shop to patronize? To put it quite bluntly, these are the two offers, made by the old-fashioned speculative builder on the one hand, and by the Garden City or Garden Suburb on the other. The exact effect upon each acre of ground is illustrated by means of Fig. 27, A, B, in

SCHEME I. ONE ACRE. SCHEME II. ONE ACRE.

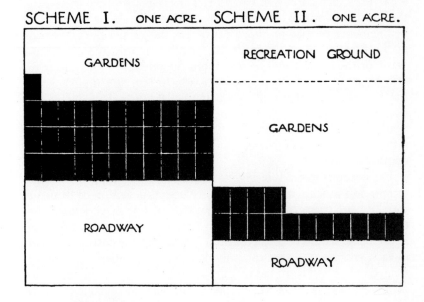

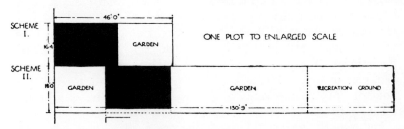

Fig. 27, A, B   A schematic summary of the principles expressed by Fig. 26, A and B, from Nothing Gained by Overcrowding!, *1912. This is the beginning of the famous Parker and Unwin slogan, "twelve to the acre."*

116

which the roadway, the houses, and the gardens are collected into separate areas. Comparing the sample acres from the two schemes, it will be seen how the space occupied by the roadway and by the additional number of houses swallows up so much of the total area of ground as to leave very little to be divided among the larger number of houses as back yard or garden for each.

The financial effect of reducing or increasing the number of houses to be placed upon a given area of ground will, of course, vary as the cost of land and road making varies.

Where the land is comparatively expensive, and road making comparatively cheap, the advantage in the price per lot to be gained by overcrowding will be greater than where land is relatively inexpensive and road making relatively dear. It is important also to distinguish between variation in the number of houses to the acre and variation in the building frontage provided to each house.

.   .   .   .

The second statement, that the return in increment to the owners of land is *reduced* by the crowding of houses to the acre instead of being increased thereby, as is generally supposed, still needs to be proved; for at first sight it will seem that, in the particular cases under consideration, the landowner was not affected by the different systems of development, because the land was assumed to be sold by him at the same price per acre in both cases. But the increment which we are considering, being the difference between the value of land for building purposes and its agricultural value, is affected not only by the price at which the land is sold, but by the quantity of land which is converted from agricultural to building uses. From this point of view let us see how the two systems of development affect the owner of a large estate upon which there is developed some new centre of population. Suppose for example, that coal is discovered under the estate, and that several coal-pits are sunk. If we assume that, as a result, there are required 6,678 new houses to accommodate the miners and their families, together with the necessary complement of professional men, tradesmen and artisans, or a total population of something like 33,000 people; if, further, we assume that the surface value of the land for agricultural purposes is £40 per acre and that its value for building purposes is £300 per acre, it will be easy to compare the result to the owner of developing all the building areas on his estate on the old-fashioned crowded system with what it would be if he adopted the Garden City method.

To accommodate 6,678 houses he will be able to sell—

$$\frac{6{,}678 \text{ houses}}{25.2 \text{ houses per acre}} = 265 \text{ acres of land, at } £300 \quad . \quad . \quad . \quad £79{,}500$$

Deduct agricultural value of 265 acres at £40 . . . . . £10,600

Gross increment [of land] due to building operations . . £68,900

If, however, having come under the influence of the Garden City Association, he should decide to limit the number of houses per acre to an average of 10.6, the result will be as follows: He will now sell—

$$\frac{6{,}678 \text{ houses}}{10.6 \text{ houses per acre}} = 630 \text{ acres of land, at } £300 \quad . \quad . \quad . \quad £189{,}000$$

Deduct the agricultural value of 630 acres at £40 . . . £ 25,200

Gross increment [of land] due to building operations . . £163,800

or an additional increment of £94,900

So long, therefore, as the estate of the owner is large enough to accommodate the whole of the development, however much it is spread out, the owner's profit or increment is reduced as the overcrowding increases. Where many owners are concerned, this would be true of the owners as a class; but it might not be true of an individual owner who might sell the whole of his land in any case. The amount of this increased increment due to the limitation of the number of houses to the acre by the Garden City method of development of course depends on whether the land is sold at the same price. There seems, however, no reason why the land should be sold at the same price, no justification for the Garden City method of development conferring this enormous increased increment value upon the owner. We have seen that increment is due to the increased value of land for building purposes, and it would seem more natural that it should be estimated rather in relation to the amount of building than in relation to the size of the garden attached to the building. It is obvious that the owner of land could afford, without loss to himself, to estimate his increment at so much per house instead of so much per acre, and where larger gardens are provided, let or sell the land at a reduced rate sufficient to recoup him first for the loss of agricultural land, secondly for the amount of increment due per house.

Let us now see at what price on these lines the owner could afford to sell the greater quantity of land required to accommodate the population we have been considering under the Garden City type of development. If the increment is to be per house instead of per acre, he will need to receive the same amount of increment in both cases, and the total sum which he ought to receive for the 630 acres would be as follows:

630 acres deducted from his agricultural land, at £40 per
    acre £25,200
Add the increment value assumed to be received . . . £68,900
                    Total £94,100

If we divide £94,100 by the 630 acres, we shall find that this represents in round figures £150 per acre. We see therefore that if the landowner in this case were willing to accept a certain increment per house, irrespective of the size of the garden, he could afford to supply the land to a Garden City Association undertaking the housing of the whole of the population springing up on his estates at the rate of £150 per acre, and be in the same position as if he had allowed the old-fashioned speculative builder to develop the land for the same population and charged £300 per acre for the land.

.   .   .   .

Fig. 28 illustrates the effect when the two Schemes are applied to a town in which an increase of population of 17,000 people takes place every year. Assuming five people to the house, that would mean 3,400 houses to be built every year. The upper half of the diagram shows the development before the adoption of a town planning scheme, the lower half shows the development after the adoption of a scheme limiting the number of houses in the same proportion we have limited them in Fig. 26B, as compared with Fig. 26A, and the figures show the total increment value and also the reduction of the price per acre which would give the same increment value in both

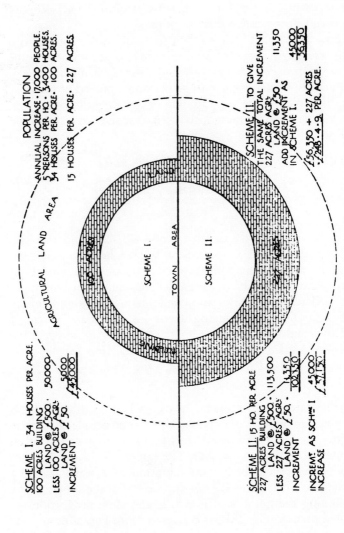

POPULATION

ANNUAL INCREASE · 17,000 PEOPLE.
5 PERSONS PER HO · 3,400 HOUSES.
34 HOUSES PER ACRE · 100 ACRES.

15 HOUSES PER ACRE · 227 ACRES

SCHEME I. 34 HOUSES PER ACRE.
100 ACRES BUILDING
    LAND @ £500 ·   50,000
LESS 100 ACRES AGR:
    LAND @ £50 ·   5,000
INCREMENT   £45,000

AGRICULTURAL LAND AREA

LAND

100 ACRES

BUILDING

SCHEME I.

TOWN AREA

SCHEME II.

227 ACRES

SCHEME II. 15 HO PER ACRE
227 ACRES BUILDING
    LAND @ £500 · 113,500
LESS 227 ACRES AGR:
    LAND @ £50 · 11,350
INCREMENT   102,150
INCREM: AS SCHE I 45,000
INCREASE   £57,150

SCHEME II TO GIVE
THE SAME TOTAL INCREMENT
227 ACRES AGR:
    LAND @ £50 · 11,350
ADD INCREMENT AS
    IN SCHEME I. 45,000
          £56,350

£56,350 ÷ 227 ACRES
= £248.4.9 PER ACRE.

Fig. 28 The effects of lower house density on the total land in a town, from Nothing Gained by Overcrowding!, 1912. The diagram was to demonstrate in the abstract how much more spread of profit or increment on "improvements" is made available to land sellers as a whole with a lower density.

cases; while the third column in Table I shows how the reduction of the price of land here arrived at would affect the cost of the individual plots.

It will be worth while at this point to consider the effect which the extra acreage required to provide for the population with the limited number of houses to the acre will have upon the size of the town; because at first sight it might be imagined that a very serious difficulty would arise in the increased distances to be travelled from the centre to the circumference. Owing, however, to the fact that the area of a circle increases not in proportion to the distance from the centre to the circumference but in proportion to the square of that distance, it follows that the increased radius required to give an area sufficient to provide each year for a given increase to the population of a town is a rapidly diminishing one: a glance at Fig. 29 will illustrate this. Further, it is probable that the application of town planning to the development of land around towns will lead to considerable economy in its use. It is only necessary to examine town maps or to move about outside the central area of any town to realize that for want of good planning there is much waste of land.

It may be useful to illustrate this question of expansion by reference to the city of London. The area of inner London administered by the London County Council represents a circle having a radius of $6\frac{1}{4}$ miles. The present population of this area is approximately 5 millions, equal to sixty-four people per acre on an average. There are still considerable areas quite unbuilt upon within this district of inner London. Supposing it possible to reduce the density of population of inner London to an average of forty-two per acre by inducing one-third of the people to live outside the boundary, let us see how this would affect the distribution of population in Greater London. The Metropolitan Police Area is approximately represented by a circle having a radius of $14\frac{3}{4}$ miles. The present population of this outer area is about 3 millions. If we were to add to this the $1\frac{2}{3}$ millions which we have assumed to be persuaded to move out we should have increased the population of Outer London to $4\frac{2}{3}$ millions of people. (See Fig. 29).

In the Hampstead Garden Suburb there will, when it is completed, be an average of something like seven houses to the acre, but the

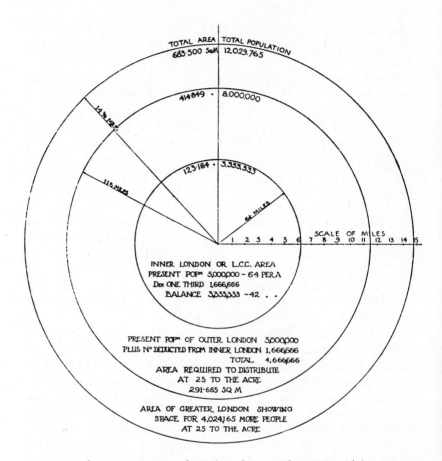

Fig. 29 Schematic Diagram of London, from Nothing Gained by Over-crowding!, *1912. This added the next Unwin perception: that the area of a circle increases in proportion to the square of the distance. The concept was that as more people were settled further out, their commuting time would be proportionately reduced in relation to their lower density. Unwin was inclined to try to attract support through such "cake and eat it" geometric theorems.*

Suburb being a residential area does not have its full proportion of land occupied by business premises and workshops. If we add to the area of the Suburb the greater part of the eighty acres of open space around which it is planned, to represent an area devoted to these purposes, we should then find that the average population to the acre would be something like twenty-five people, equivalent to about five houses. Assuming that the $4\frac{2}{3}$ millions of population, which we have considered should be provided for in Greater London, were to be spread out on this basis of an average of twenty-five to the acre, I find that including the population supposed to be left in inner London, the total of 8,000,000 people would only need an area having a radius of $11\frac{1}{2}$ miles, while the present area of Greater London would allow of the population increasing from eight millions up to twelve millions distributed on this same basis.

It will be seen, therefore, that the total additional distance to be travelled as a result of preventing overcrowding is a comparatively unimportant matter. Indeed overcrowding, though very bad in certain areas, is very much a local evil, and it is remarkable to find how small is the average number of people to the acre in many districts of London, where one knows that the overcrowding on certain individual acres is very bad. We may, therefore, safely say that there is no sound argument against reducing the number of houses to the acre on the score of seriously increasing the distances to be travelled.

It may well be asked, how is it if the economic advantages of overcrowding are so small and the disadvantages so great that the overcrowding system has so generally been adopted? The reason is simply this, that the one person who can secure the advantage happens to be the person who is generally able to settle the type of development, namely, the individual who, having a limited plot of land, sets out to secure the maximum return he can from it by building upon it; and it is true that the value of land as a definite stand for a building is greater than its value as garden land around the same building. In the case of the owners of land, the reason is probably due to the fact that they have not thoroughly thought out or understood the matter, and have looked at the price per individual acre, and have not realised, for example, that if they could sell two acres of land for £300 every year, they were doing better than if they sold one acre of land for £500. But, unfortunately, the majority of people, and particularly the occupants of small houses, which are the ones usually most overcrowded, care chiefly to get a house of some sort at the least cost, and have no means of knowing, because no choice is ever put before them by which they may judge, that they are paying at an extravagantly high rate for their small plots as compared with what they might pay for much larger plots.

. . . .

So long as each individual speculative builder looks at his own acre of land only, having bought it and paid the price for it, it is probable that he can sweat out of that land a little more profit by building the maximum number of houses upon it, because in spite of the increased cost of development, under present circumstances the return, whether he sells the land or lets the houses, will increase a little the more buildings he puts upon it, and increase a little faster than the increase in the cost of development. But if the number of houses to the acre around a growing town is limited under a town planning scheme, this does not mean that the builders will get less profit in the future. It may mean that an individual speculator, who has bought an individual plot, will make less profit out of that particular piece of land than he would have done, though, as has been shown, the difference will be very much less than he imagines. He need not, however, lose anything of his profit per house, because the same number of houses will be required; and though it may re-quire a little more capital to purchase enough land for the same num-ber of houses, there seems no reason to suppose that the limitation of the number of houses to the acre is in any way liable to reduce the builder's profit either on the buildings themselves or on the increased value of the land due to development, if this profit is estimated per house, as it should be, and not per acre, as at present is the custom. And we have seen that this is true for the owner of land also. In spite, therefore, of the fears of the landowner and the speculative builder there does not seem to be any reason why town planning should not prove to be to the real benefit of both parties.

. . . .

Experience has shown that where plots have been laid out by a land owner, not of the minimum size, and where they have been let at a fixed ground rent, it is very difficult to induce the speculative builder to erect upon them small cottages, even where the demand for small cottages is very great. In many towns, of which Cardiff affords a notable instance, it will be found that the builder has erected upon each plot a large type of cottage, having three rooms and a scullery on the ground floor and three or four bedrooms on the first floor. This large house is so costly that the workman cannot afford to pay the whole of the rent himself, and is therefore forced to take in another family to lodge in part of the house to help pay the rent. I think it is of great importance, therefore, when limiting the number of houses to the acre, whether this is done by a town planning scheme or by an individual owner leasing or selling land for building purposes, that the reduction of the number of houses to the acre should not be by means of a simple flat rate of ten or twelve, but should be in accordance with a scale bearing a relation to the size of the house. In this way only can the tendency to build larger houses than are required in any district be checked, and in this way only can the excessive overcrowding of the medium and larger sized house in places where there is a great demand for them be prevented. In several cases of development on Garden City and Garden Suburb lines, in order to secure that too large buildings should not be erected on the more generous sized plots there provided, it has been necessary to fix for each plot a maximum size of building to be erected upon it.

.   .   .   .

In framing the regulations at the Garden City at Letchworth it was sought to meet this point to some extent by the following provisions:

1. That in the case of houses on ordinary sites, not more than one-sixth of the site should be covered by buildings.
2. That dwelling houses costing less than £200 should not exceed 12 to the acre; houses costing from £200 to £300 should not exceed 10 to the acre; houses costing from £300 to £350 should not exceed 8 to the acre; and so forth.

These regulations being framed under the Company's lease, it was possible to allow more discretion in their interpretation and application than would be practicable if they were to be enforced by Local Authorities as building regulations under a town planning scheme. But it is suggested the difficulty may be met by some such arrangement. Certainly to limit to a fixed amount, say ten or fifteen, for example, the number of houses irrespective of size which may be erected on the acre, would be a very rough and ready way of securing the ends desired; and the alternative method which has been suggested of limiting the number of cubic feet of building to the acre, although accommodating itself more scientifically to one aspect of the subject, is nearly as crude as the previously mentioned flat rate limitation, because quite unrelated to another aspect. The fact is that there are two important and different considerations which make some sort of limitation desirable. One has relation to the amount of building and the other has relation to the population, and the desired end can only be attained by some scale which takes into account both these relations.

A limitation of the cubic contents of the building would have the effect of requiring one acre of ground for a single house when it reached a certain size, and that not a very large size, if at the same time, it was to have the effect of preventing more than ten to fifteen families living on the acre. For the purposes of general amenity, a certain amount of open space in relation to cubic size of building is desirable; but, on the other hand, it is perhaps even more desirable that there should be sufficient area of open ground for garden and recreation purposes for each family, irrespective of the size of the house it occupies. It is for this reason that I think a scale of limiting the number of houses to the acre would be found to be on the whole simplest and most satisfactory. Such scale can be arranged to allow sufficient space in proportion to the increased cubic size of larger houses, and at the same time provide for the proportionately larger area of garden per family, which is desirable as compared with the cubic size of the smaller types of cottages.

It has the additional advantage of following closely the lines laid down in the Housing and Town Planning, etc., Act, 1909, which permits "restrictions on the number of buildings which may be erected on each acre, and the height and character of those buildings."

8

Higher Building
in Relation to Town Planning

*Read before the Royal Institute of British Architects,
Monday, 17 December 1923*

HERE was once a great controversy which, I believe, profoundly moved the theological world of its day, if it did not even threaten the peace of empires, as to how many angels could stand on a needle's point. To-day we look back with wonder, not perhaps untinged with some slight contempt, that serious people could have spent their energies in such a discussion.

But examining, as I have been constrained to do during the last twenty or thirty years, the attempts which mankind is making in various parts of the world to find out, not how many ethereal angels, but how many ponderous people and still more ponderous motor-cars can occupy the same square yard of ground at the same time, I begin to wonder whether the superiority of our intelligence to that of our theologically minded forefathers is as obvious as we should like to think!

Twenty or thirty years ago in this country it was generally assumed that great gains could be secured by overcrowding dwellings upon the land; that some dire economic necessity arising from these reputed gains compelled us so to develop our towns. That fallacy has now been pretty well exploded. Most of those who have examined the matter are agreed that, if people will, land can be developed at a density of ten or twelve houses to the acre at little, if any, more, and sometimes at even less cost per house, than the same land can be developed for the same type of house, at a density of twenty or thirty to the acre; that so far from there being anything to be gained from overcrowding dwellings on land, the fact is that such overcrowding yields less total return to the landowners, and affords a dearer plot

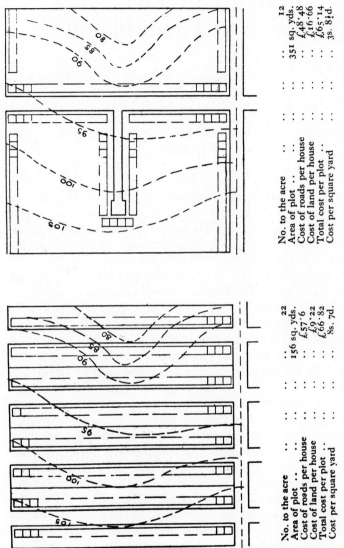

					12
No. to the acre	..	..	..	..	351 sq. yds.
Area of plot ..	..	..	..	..	£48·48
Cost of roads per house	..	..	..	£16·66
Cost of land per house	..	..	..	£65·14
Total cost per plot ..	..	..	..	3s. 8½d.
Cost per square yard					

					22
No. to the acre	..	..	..	..	156 sq. yds.
Area of plot ..	..	..	..	..	£57·6
Cost of roads per house	..	..	..	£9·22
Cost of land per house	..	..	..	£66·82
Total cost per plot ..	..	..	..	8s. 7d.
Cost per square yard					

Fig. 30, A, B   The fully developed "twelve to the acre" idiom, from "Higher Building in Relation to Town Planning," 1924. The cul-de-sac is the new feature (in contrast to Fig. 26B) and is only a diagrammatic exploration since almost always in practice it was used to penetrate odd-shaped, not rectilinear lots.

128

for the occupant (Fig. 30A, B. See also Fig. 26A, B). So that apart from other disadvantages, congestion of dwellings is really an expensive luxury. Unable to believe, however, anything so simple as that there is plenty of room for everybody; that it is crowding, the attempt of two people to stand on a space that is only large enough for one, which causes most of our urban difficulties; modern business intelligence is now proposing to adopt vertical overcrowding. Unless we are careful, it will not be content without actual and disastrous demonstration that this particular form of overcrowding has even less to be said for it than the horizontal kind. The fact that this method has been fairly well tested in America; that it has created there urban problems of a difficulty exceeding anything which we know even in this great city; that 183 American towns containing 40 per cent. of the urban population have already adopted zoning ordinances, and that the remaining cities are hurrying after one another pell-mell to adopt regulations limiting the height of buildings, as drastic as the vested interests already created will allow, does not seem enough to convince some of our urban theologians that many men cannot stand on the same flagstone at the same time, or more than one car move at one moment on an identical piece of roadway. Nevertheless, in the hope that it is not too late to save our London from copying mistakes which New York, Chicago, and other American cities now regret, and the evil results of which they are now desperately struggling to remove, it seems worth while to examine somewhat carefully the conditions which prevail in those cities, and to realise what would be the effect in London if we were to adopt the method of expansion upwards which the Americans are trying to check.

The arguments that can be brought against the adoption of high buildings are many and weighty. The law of diminishing returns applies to such buildings in almost all respects. With every added storey the effective floor area per storey is reduced, while the cost per square foot is increased; the greater proportional number of lifts required take their toll of space from each of an increasing number of floors. You do not dispense with transportation by going up; you merely change the horizontally moving omnibus for the vertically travelling lift, and incidentally make walking for even short journeys far more difficult.

One witness before the New York Height of Buildings Commission calculated that the average time taken to reach the 30th floor would equal that of taking the express train on the subway to a spot one mile distant.

The same law holds good as to light. Every storey added tends to darken all the floors below. In spite of the bright light of New York, the number of dark rooms in which artificial light must always be used is far greater than with us. The consequent injury to health and loss of efficiency is said to be serious; eyesight is injured; tuberculosis and other diseases are encouraged. Much evidence was also given showing that high buildings lead to unstable property values. They unduly inflate the price of land and concentrate property development in small areas where the maintenance of values is very speculative, thus preventing a more widely distributed and stable improvement. The values of the lower rooms in adjacent buildings, whether themselves high or low, are depreciated by the erection of higher buildings which diminish their light and obstruct their ventilation. It is true that one advocate of higher buildings gave as his reason the pleasure of living on the highest floors; but he overlooked the fact that the higher the buildings the smaller must be the proportion of people who can have the benefit of living at the top.

I do not propose to enlarge on these or other similar arguments to-night because the conclusive argument against high buildings is that no real gain to the community is secured by adopting them. As hitherto used, they have so far deprived each other of light and air, and so seriously congested the traffic in the streets, as largely to destroy their own value and to deprive themselves of reasonably comfortable access even if they could be spaced so far apart as to allow proper light and air, and if the streets could be laid out of such widths as to carry their concentrated traffic without congestion, the total area covered would then be little, if any, less than that required to provide for the same community with buildings of normal height.

This more general or town planning aspect of the problem has acquired a special degree of urgency for us during the last few years, because we appear to be following another lead of our American cousins in regard to the extensive use of the private motor-car. We are following far behind American attainments, but still evidently following. In that country there are something like twelve million cars, or an average of about one car for every ten people, including men, women, and children. There are, moreover, several individual towns in which the number of cars registered has risen to one for every five of the population. In some of these towns it has been calculated that there is seating accommodation in these cars for the whole of the population to go joy riding at the same time!

It is not yet apparent what will prove to be the saturation point in regard to ownership of motorcars. Mr. Ford, who has contributed more than anyone else to the supply, does not consider that that point has been nearly reached; and I am informed that the industry in America is at the present time turning out approximately half a million cars per month. While they export a good many, the majority are for the supply of their own population. We in this country have little idea what this means. We still number our total possession of cars in hundreds of thousands, and our annual output in tens of thousands. While we may hope, as much for the pleasure of the motor-car owner as for the safety of foot passengers, that we shall not reach numbers comparable with those found in America, there is yet little doubt that our present number will expand enormously. It is increasing even in the present time of depression at a rate approaching 25 per cent. per annum. We must therefore reckon with a rapidly extending use of the private motor-car as one of the conditions which must be dealt with in the future. There is little evidence that this condition is likely to be accompanied by any diminution in other kinds of vehicles, such as the motor omnibus, which is already threatening to present one of our most serious traffic problems.

To understand the traffic aspect of the high building question it is necessary first to realise the extent to which an increase in the height of buildings affects the demand on street space. Fortunately this problem of height has recently been investigated with great care by the Chicago Real Estate Board, in connection with the fixing of height limits throughout that city. In their report they give precise data for buildings ranging from five to thirty storeys high, erected on one particular corner plot, including the net rentable floor space, cost, and other matters. There appears to be a fairly constant relation between the net rentable floor space and the total day population. I have checked it in connection with one or two individual buildings like the Woolworth Building in New York, and also in connection with the whole of the Loop area of Chicago, and I find that a figure of about 45 square feet of rentable floor per head of population appears to be near the mark. To be on the safe side I propose, in my calculations, to take 50 square feet of net floor space per head of population —that is, total day population. It is quite simple to establish a definite relation between this population and the footpath area of the roads, and for this purpose I have assumed that, to provide standing room, a space 2 feet by 2 feet is necessary for each person; and to provide for walking, on the average a space of 2 feet by 5 feet is necessary. It will be realised that crowds of people walking along a footpath rarely average so little space as this. It is not possible to establish a definite relation between the road surface and all the various vehicles required to serve buildings of different height; but as we have in America a fairly reliable relation between population and the number of motor-cars owned, it is easy to establish a relation between the floor space of the buildings and the road space that would be required to accommodate these motor-cars; this relation is sufficient for my purpose. The average over-all length of a number of motor vehicles, I find, is 20 feet; and allowing a little space for the cars to stand clear of each other, about 24 or 25 feet is as little as can be allowed for each car. I have further assumed that the cars occupy a width of road space varying from 7 feet 6 inches to 8 feet, according as the carriage-way most nearly divides up into a certain number of car widths. These densities of occupancy of foot-way and road are illustrated in Fig. 31. The building which is taken for comparison of different heights was designed to stand on a corner plot in the Loop area, measuring 160 feet by 172 feet, with an alley-way at the rear. With five storeys I find that this building would have a day population of 2,018, and taking the average width of the road-ways in the Loop area, which is about 86 feet, and the footway in front of the building as one-fifth of this, or 17 feet, I find that the people occupying this one building would take up a length of 504 feet of footway if they were standing, and a length of 1,260 feet if they were walking. It has been observed that the average speed of people walking on the footway in a crowded condition comparable to this would be 224 feet per minute, so that this length of 1,260 feet of footway would be occupied for five and a half minutes before the occupants of this one building could pass away from it. If the building were increased to ten storeys the population would not be doubled—that is, 4,036—but would be about 3,704, and the length of footway to accommodate this number walk-

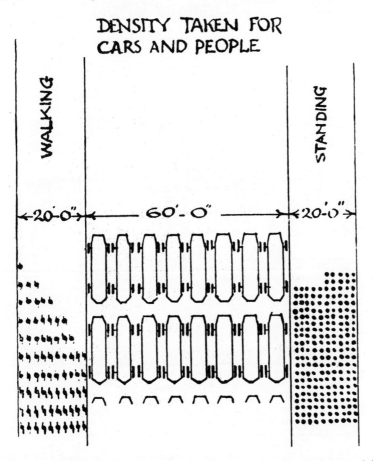

Fig. 31 Comparative density of people walking or standing and automobiles, from "Higher Building in Relation to Town Planning," 1924. This would refer to the Loop Area of Chicago and the Woolworth Building.

133

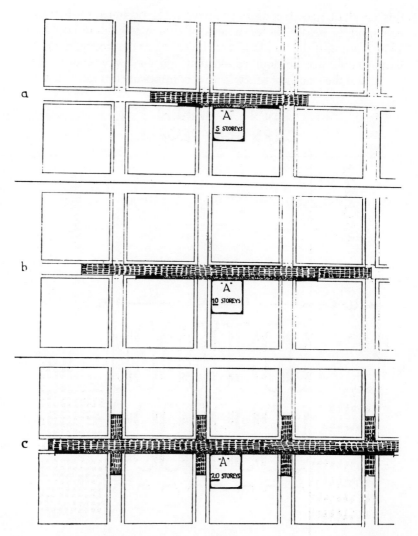

Fig. 32   Amount of street required for automobiles and pedestrians if a building is five, ten or twenty stories, from "Higher Building in Relation to Town Planning," 1924. This was the kind of illustration Unwin cherished, abstract but fraught with meaning.

ing would be 2,315 feet. The time in this case for the people to pass would be ten minutes. With an increase to twenty storeys the figures would be—population accommodated, 6,930; length of footway occupied, 4,330 feet; time to pass, 20 minutes. Above twenty storeys, owing to the large amount of floor space occupied by lifts on the lower floors, the increase of available space in proportion to the number of added floors becomes steadily smaller, so that at thirty storeys, instead of a floor space enough to provide for 12,114 persons, the population would only be about 9,368; the length of footway occupied by even this number would, however, be 5,853 feet, or considerably over a mile; and the time required for the people to pass any point on that footway would be nearly half an hour.

Turning now to the conditions in the carriage-way; it is safe to assume in America that the class of people which forms the day population in city buildings, including as it does a minimum proportion of children and others not owning cars, will at any rate own the average number of one car to every ten people. On this basis, if these cars were to attend at the building to bring people to work or take them away in the evening, and were packed as closely as already indicated, they would fill the whole of carriage-way for a length of 804 feet with a five storey building, 1,480 feet with a ten storey building, 2,772 feet with a twenty storey building, and 3,744 feet, nearly three-quarters of a mile, with a thirty storey building. These lengths of road required are also illustrated in Fig. 32. If half the carriage-way only were taken, on the ground that the other half of the street should be left for the use of the buildings on the other side, these lengths would have to be doubled; it may reasonably be said, therefore, that with the present extent of ownership of motors in America, the cars require nearly twice as much length of roadway to accommodate them as the people would require walking along the footways. We must not forget, in considering these figures, that no account has been taken of the increase of other vehicles, particularly trade vehicles, required to deal with the growing volume of merchandise that would be handled by the increasing population. It is, perhaps, not necessary to take account of the increase in motor omnibuses and other similar vehicles, because we have reckoned the whole of the people as either walking or riding in cars. On the other hand, it is a well-known principle, which applies as far as I know generally in all towns, that the extent of public passenger traffic increases much faster than the increase of population. In fact, the increase of traffic and of the number of journeys per head is frequently more than the square of the increase of population. That has been so both in London and New York. To the extent to which this holds true, Fig. 32 understates the increasing demand on the streets due to increase in height.

We may take one more example in connection with which accurate information is available. I refer to the Woolworth Building in New York (Fig. 33). This building stands on a plot 151 feet by 195 feet; it has streets on three sides of it; it has, including basement, 28 storeys covering the whole area of the building apart from lighting wells, and has, further, a tower containing a like number of additional storeys. The day population of the building is 14,000 people.

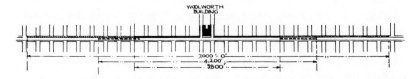

Fig. 33 The sidewalk area and roadway required for 14,000 occupants of the Woolworth Building and their cars, over a mile and a quarter. From "Higher Building in Relation to Town Planning," 1924. This concept was the basis of the well-known, and later enlarged, argument that if all the people were let out of all the skyscrapers at once, there would be no room in the streets.

In addition to this there are large numbers of visitors that I have not reckoned. The roadway in front of it is less than 100 feet, but for convenience we will take the usual New York main avenue width of 100 feet, having footways 20 feet wide and a 60-feet carriage-way. On the bases we have taken, therefore, the footway would accommodate a maximum of ten persons walking abreast, and I have assumed that the carriage-way would take eight motor-cars abreast, allowing only 7 feet 6 inches per car. The day population of this one building would therefore occupy 2,800 feet of side-walk standing packed together, or, if walking, 7,000 feet—over a mile and a quarter; and they would occupy a minimum of half an hour in passing over any part of that space. . . .

Assuming, again, one car for ten people, and that the whole of the roadway were occupied, the cars would require 4,200 feet of roadway to provide standing room. Should it be arranged for these cars to draw up at the door of the building to take their owners home, allowing an average length for car and space to move of 25 feet, the queue of cars in single file would be between six and seven miles long.

In view of these figures you will hardly be surprised that the utility of the private car is diminishing, or wonder at the enormous congestion of traffic in cities like New York and Chicago. It is only because the very tall building is quite exceptional in New York, and even on Manhattan Island is confined to very restricted areas, that an absolute deadlock has not already been reached. The vast majority of buildings, even in the downtown area, as may be seen from a recent aeroplane photograph, are still of the old height of five or six storeys. Even as it is, the problem of traffic is almost insoluble. Along Fifth Avenue it is now regulated by signal lights. When the white light shows, the stream flows along the avenue; when the green light shows, the traffic along the whole length of the avenue thus controlled must stop at every cross street. These cross streets occur at intervals of only 88 yards centre to centre, and the whole of the traffic must stop with the signal, whether any vehicle requires to cross the street or not. It is not often that at any of the cross streets there is nothing waiting, but as the whole of the stream must be stopped long enough on the average to allow the traffic of the busiest cross streets to pass, it must be held longer than necessary at all the less busy cross streets. The arrangement is, however, in spite of these drawbacks, considered to be a great improvement on the previous condition.

The difficulty of dealing with the foot passengers is no less than that of the road traffic (Fig. 34). It is estimated that the subways could deal, as a maximum, with 60,000 people per hour, if they could get that number to the trains. But we have already seen that the 14,000 people from the Woolworth Building would themselves occupy over a mile and a quarter of one of New York's main footways, and it would take them half an hour to enter the station. The congestion at the entrances to the tube stations under these circumstances can hardly

Fig. 34 People leaving a New York skyscraper at evening, from "Higher Build-ing in Relation to Town Planning," 1924. Even in a wide street the congestion is heavy, and the antlike scale of the humans in contrast to the huge buildings only emphasizes the loneliness to be found among the crowds of the vast city. The lonely crowd and forgotten man atmosphere of the 1920's and 1930's, often remarked by sociologists, novelists, and movie makers, was probably not a false one. It had been building up physically for over a century in the great cities. But the increased mobility, as here, concealed it as a mass, instead of an individual, phenomenon.

138

be surprising, but this is not the worst. The condition has been reached when it is doubtful whether any relief can be secured by constructing new tube railways. Even with the present limits of height allowed under the recent zoning laws, I was informed by the engineer in charge of these railways, and the figures we have looked at confirm this, that buildings may and probably would be erected on two or three blocks adjacent to any new tube station, the population of which would fill the railway for the best part of an hour at the busiest time of the day. The total congestion, in fact, might easily be increased instead of being relieved by the new facilities. The advocates of higher buildings seem to take the view that it is the business of the public authorities who are responsible for the streets to find accommodation for any amount of traffic which their buildings may originate. Some of them, it is true, suggest that the owners might agree to a strictly moderate set-back of their building for every increased storey in height. What general benefit this would afford beyond a little local relief in front of the building itself is not very clear, particularly in view of the length of footway, far exceeding the length of the building, which we have seen is required to provide bare standing space for the occupants of the high buildings. Many times even that length must be congested by those occupants before the volume of traffic is dissipated. But it will be well to prove the futility of such suggestions by showing what extra space would actually be involved. For this purpose I cannot do better than take the conditions in the central area of Chicago, which is locally known as the Loop because it is roughly contained within the loop lines of the overhead railways. Full particulars are available in regard to this area, and being regularly planned on the chequer-board system it is easy to reduce conditions to diagrammatic form. This area is one of the most congested in the world; although many of the buildings—those coloured red on the plan—exceed twelve, and some of them—coloured blue—exceed seventeen storeys in height, there are no skyscrapers rivalling the Woolworth and the Equitable of New York; the average height for the whole area has been estimated as equal to seven storeys.

I have had some recent experience of the conditions of traffic in this district, and there can be no question that the streets, although they represent about forty per cent. of the total area of the ground, are quite inadequate to carry the present traffic with reasonable despatch, let alone comfort. I am satisfied that they would be taxed to the limit of comfortable conditions if the average were five storeys instead of seven. Neglecting the cumulative increase in traffic which

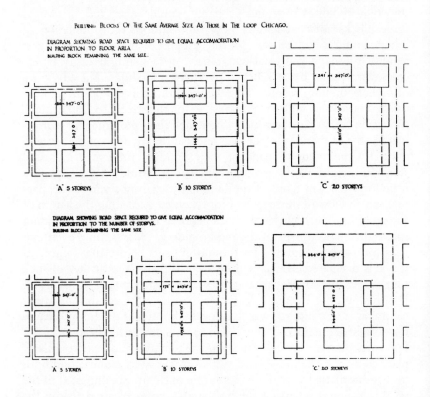

Fig. 35   Diagrams to show how much roadway buildings of five, ten and twenty stories require, the building block size remaining the same, from "Higher Building in Relation to Town Planning." The contrast was to show how much service space was logically needed, even if not available, for the higher structures. Wider streets slowed down traffic, because of the equal American intersections taking pedestrians and cars longer to cross. This was also involved with the proper phasing of stoplights, as Unwin duly noted.

universal experience shows to arise from increased population, and assuming that full value is obtained by increasing the area of roads *pro rata* with the increase of the density of population, I have calculated the roads that would be required to give the same relative accommodation if the average height of the buildings were increased from the assumed five to ten and to twenty storeys. In the first instance, keeping the average size of the building block the same, I find that for ten-storey buildings to give the same ratio of street area to net floor accommodation as at present, the widths of the road would have to be increased from their present average of 86 feet to an average of 144 feet; and if the storeys were increased to twenty, the width of the streets would require to be 241 feet. Figure 35 shows a few of these blocks to illustrate this point. If the increasing intensity of traffic were assumed to balance the loss of floor space, and its volume were taken to expand *pro rata* with the increased number of floors, which is probably nearer to the actual truth, a still greater increase of road areas would be required. It will be noticed that if such an expansion of road space had to be applied to the whole Loop area, in order to accommodate traffic resulting from the increased height of buildings, it would be necessary to pull down a considerable part of the town surrounding this area to provide the additional land required! It is obvious, however, that any such increase in the width of the roads, even on the more modest scale first shown, would be impracticable, and that if it were attempted the traffic would not in fact be relieved to a degree anything approaching the extent of the increase. The delay at every crossing for vehicles, and still more for foot passengers, owing to the increased width of the streets, would be very great. This is already noticeable to an Englishman in New York, where most of the north and south avenues are 100 feet, and the cross streets 64 feet, wide. The time occupied in crossing these many streets, and the extra delay to traffic in consequence, is obviously a serious factor, as compared with the conditions in the City of London, for example.

But suppose, instead of keeping the building block the same size, we try to follow literally the suggestion of some of the advocates of high buildings in this country, and provide sufficient additional road space by means of a set-back, thus reducing the size of the building block. How then should we fare? This also has been tested. Taking the same bases of calculation as before, and assuming that the additional accommodation required is equal to the increase of the total available building area from five to ten storeys, I find, in order to provide the necessary set-back around one of the average blocks in the Loop, that the reduction in the size of the building to allow for extra width of road enough to maintain a constant relation between floor space and road area would just about represent the area provided in an additional five storeys; so that instead of increasing the building from five to ten storeys, the building would be required to be increased to fifteen storeys to provide the required accommodation. In other words, if the owner of the aspiring building is to provide adjacent only to his own frontage an addition to the existing road space *pro rata* to the increase of net available floor area, his loss of land will be so great that he will have to add double the number of floors that would have been required on his original area! Even then only the roads adjacent to the building block would have been widened.

If the difficulty of accommodating the pedestrian and the moving traffic is great, the case of the standing motor-car is even worse. Of the 60,000 motor-cars which the present occupants of the Loop own among them, only 3,500 can find places where standing is permitted within the Loop area (Fig. 36). If the whole of the road space were packed solid with cars, there would still be only standing room for 11,000 cars, or something like one-fifth of those owned. As a matter of fact, the car owners of the Loop area have appropriated the large open space between Michigan Avenue and the Lake, set aside for Grant Park, and it is no uncommon thing to see 25,000 motor-cars, or more than twice the number that would fill the streets of the Loop, parked at one time on this gigantic motor garage. Indeed, the promoters of the great town-planning scheme designed by Daniel Burnham, of which this park is a conspicuous feature, are not free from anxiety as to how they are to recover this area from the motor owners to lay it out and plant it.

Owing to the fact that the motor-car is mainly used in America by people who do not employ a chauffeur, the question of parking the cars already presents an unsolved problem. The difficulty is felt especially in the more congested areas, where it has had to be solved by forbidding cars to stand for more than a few minutes, and then only in the less frequented streets, which means that the majority of car owners can no longer use them for going to and from their work. Even in small cities, however, it is becoming a serious problem; and plans of city improvements now indicate not only the lines of traffic provided for, but also the amount of space left over for parking cars against the sidewalk. It is common in cities of quite moderate size to have to drive round several blocks, or along several streets, before a space can be found in which to park the car. Anybody going from business to his club to lunch may frequently find that in walking to the car and back again, and walking from the nearest parking space to the club and back again, he has travelled a greater distance than if he had walked in the first instance from his business to the club!

Without pursuing this matter further, enough has, I hope, been said to prove the main contention which I put forward to-night—that increase in height of buildings necessarily involves augmented

Fig. 36 Michigan Avenue, North of Randolph Street, before improvement, from "Higher Building in Relation to Town Planning," 1924.

143

street traffic; that where the traffic has already reached the comfortable capacity of the streets, any further increase in height must cause or increase congestion, with consequent loss of time and efficiency for all the users of the street. Further, that this increase cannot in practice be met by street widening, because the utmost that can be done in this direction can barely cope with the other causes which in all growing modern towns are tending to swell the volume of street traffic.

Increased height, therefore, means increased traffic congestion. It is urgent that we in London should realise this while there is yet time, and most important that we should compare our circumstances with those in America, where we may observe the traffic conditions which are likely to arise here in a few years.

For this purpose we may compare the conditions which we have been examining in the Loop area at Chicago with those in the City of London. The areas are in many ways comparable; each is the main commercial centre of a great city; the City of London, which has an area of about a square mile, is the heart of a town and urbanized region the total population of which approaches nine millions; the Loop area in Chicago, about one-third of a square mile, is equally the centre of a total population well over three millions; both areas are served by numerous railways, street cars, etc., and contain a large, number of official and commercial buildings, retail stores, and warehouses; one is bounded on the south side by the River Thames, the other on the east side by Lake Michigan. The City of London contains about 638 acres, the Loop in Chicago only about 212 acres; the day population of the City of London is about 416,000, or 614 persons to the acre; the day population of the Loop is about 600,000, or 2,830 persons to the acre; in Chicago the total streets represent about 40 per cent. of the area; in London, including private back streets, only about 28 per cent.; in Chicago few of the streets are less than 46 feet wide, some of them are over 100 feet, and the average width is 86 feet; in the City of London the average width of the streets, including some which are footways only, is about 28 feet. In spite of the relatively liberal provision of sidewalks on these wide streets in Chicago, it is quite common at busy times to see the foot passengers swarming off the footway until they occupy the whole of the street area from side to side, and completely stop for the time being all vehicular traffic. At other times, the queues of vehicles waiting to pass some of the important crossings accumulate to such an extent that the rearmost vehicles in the queue may have to wait three times before they are able to pass one of these crossings. In other words, the queue becomes more than twice as long as can be allowed to pass during the few minutes' interval that it is practicable to hold up the opposite stream of traffic.

These conditions have arisen from the intensive use of a limited number of tall buildings from ten to twenty storeys high, sufficient only to raise the average height over the whole area available for building to seven storeys. If the land in the City of London should ever be used to the same degree of intensity, and sufficient high buildings were allowed to give an average of seven storeys as in the Loop, I estimate that the day population would be 1,845,000, instead of the present 416,150. In that case the narrow streets of the City would have to carry four or five times the present volume of traffic, which is already far in excess of their comfortable capacity. We must realise that if not one single storey is added to any building in the City of London, the increased use of the private motor car and other causes will increase the traffic in the area to a very serious extent.

Unfortunately I have come across no evidence that the increasing use of the private motor-car causes a diminution in the patronage of public means of conveyance. On the contrary, experience shows that this demand for public transportation facilities is still rapidly growing. The increasing extent to which the streets of London are now being occupied by the motor omnibus must be apparent to everybody, and the lengthening queues of these 'buses which accumulate on important road crossings already present a formidable appearance. It is clear, therefore, that, quite apart from any increase in the height or volume of buildings within the central area of London, we are likely to have to face a steadily increasing volume of private and public transportation on the streets. It will tax all our powers to provide adequate road space to deal with this traffic, without permitting any increase in the height of buildings, with the consequent further congestion of people and business in the centre.

The advocates of high buildings suggest that their policy would at any rate reduce the general traffic problem. I find no evidence to support this, and much that tends the other way. If the concentration of people in high business and residence buildings tended to reduce traffic, a comparison of the traffic conditions in New York with those in decentralised London should give some indication of this. On the contrary, the number of journeys per head of the population in New York exceeds 500 per annum, considerably more than in London, where last year they numbered 390.

It is true that Mr. Frank Pick, from whose recent Paper read at the London School of Economics I am quoting these and some of the following figures, estimated that the journeys per head this year will reach 414. This will indeed be a striking testimony to his genius for stimulating traffic by fascinating pictorial advertisements, aided a little perhaps by the abnormal shortage of houses, which obliges a larger proportion of the population than usual to live in the wrong place. But even that figure, if reached, is well below the New York number; and I have no doubt there are counterparts to Mr. Pick at work boosting up the number in that enterprising city also.

The amount of cross traffic in London is enormous; it is estimated that 60 per cent. of the whole population engaged in business or labour in the area live in one place and work in another; while for all purposes something like three million people converge on the central areas daily.

Last year I spent some time consulting with the committee who are preparing a new plan for Greater New York on this and similar problems, and was impressed by the fact that the multiplication of dwellings and of business premises, in the centre, due to high buildings, so far from relieving the strain upon traffic, tends considerably to increase that strain. Moreover, there was no evidence that any economy in the space covered by the town or the distances which had to be travelled, was secured as a result of the concentration in high buildings; and certainly no reduction was apparent in the time occupied in travelling about the town or to outlying suburbs. This came somewhat as a surprise. Like most casual visitors, I had not realised how small a proportion of New York is represented by Manhattan Island, nor had I previously experienced the very long railway journeys necessary to reach some of the New York suburbs. If circles having a radius of 5 and 10 miles respectively are drawn on the maps of London and New York the result is somewhat surprising. Undoubtedly a considerable proportion of the area which falls within the circles as applied to New York is occupied by water; but on the other hand a very large area of the town falls outside the outer circle; whereas the bulk of the built-up area of London is included within the inner circle; and most of the further suburbs, such as Ealing, Hendon, Woodford, Ilford, Woolwich, Bromley, with the larger part of Croydon, Merton and Richmond, fall well within the outer circle. Chicago also occupies a remarkably large area. The territory of the town itself extends for a length of 26 miles, with a width varying from 6 to 9 miles. Outside that area there are considerable suburbs, such as Evanston and Winnetka in the north, and the important industrial area known as Gary to the south-east. It is not easy altogether to explain the large areas covered. A much greater street width is provided in American cities, and this has a cumulative effect on the expansion of the town, as is apparent in Fig. 35. Moreover, owing to the fact that the area of a town varies not in proportion to the diameter but in proportion to the square of the diameter, a difference of density of dwellings, or of occupancy generally, has less effect on the distance travelled from the suburbs to the centre than would be expected (Fig. 37).

These considerations go some way to explain why the more general use of high buildings leads to little, if any, reduction in the size of American towns. A consideration of our own habits will suggest why they lead to an increase rather than a reduction in the demand on traffic facilities. About 13,455 people who work in London are brought in every day from Southend, 35 miles out. Let us examine the relative transport facilities which these people require, as compared with those which they would need if they were added to the population adjacent to the central area by increasing the height of the buildings there situated. Instead of 13,000 odd people taking one journey to and from their work in the day, and an occasional extra journey connected with their business, is it not clear that if they were living in the centre, they and their families would be on and off the various means of transport all through the day; that the extra tradesmen with their delivery vans; the postmen, milkmen, doctors, and all the other people attending to their daily wants, would enormously swell the volume of traffic in the central streets? Instead of 13,000 odd persons being carried twice or three times in a day, a population of four or five times that number would be utilising the streets and all the various means of public transport the whole day through. I venture to suggest that, contrary to the view of the advocates of high buildings, it is approximately true to say that in regard to a large town, the

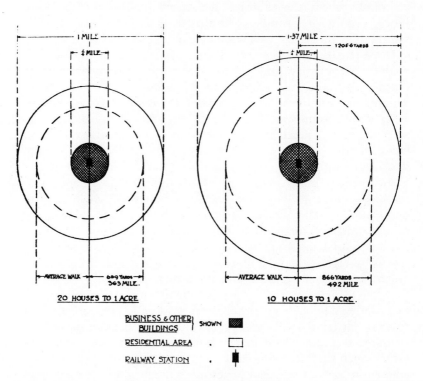

20 HOUSES TO 1 ACRE   10 HOUSES TO 1 ACRE.

BUSINESS & OTHER BUILDINGS } SHOWN ▨

RESIDENTIAL AREA . ▢

RAILWAY STATION . ▮

Showing the average length of walk to a railway station as affected by the density of dwellings

Density, i.e., No. of houses to the acre	Average size of Plot	Average walk to station
10	420 sq. yds.	866 yds.
20	185 sq. yds.	639 yds.

Density doubled ; length of walk reduced 26 per cent.

Fig. 37 Circular diagram to show relative distances to railroad station with twenty and ten houses to the acre, from "Higher Building in Relation to Town Planning," 1924. This is another version of Figs. 28, 29.

nearer people live to the centre, the greater is the demand which is made on the street and the various public transport conveniences, and the farther they live from the centre, the less is that demand. Anyone who will consider the ways of his own family and those who serve them, will confirm this.

The real transport difficulty in connection with the residents in Southend and similar places is of quite a different nature. It is not so much a question of congesting the traffic in the centre, as one of the cost of providing adequate transport facilities at the two busy times, when folk are going to or from their work, in cases where the demand for transport during the remaining hours of the day falls far below the peak load. This problem is by no means insoluble. The chief difficulty springs from the capital cost of the permanent way, which may have to be spread over a short daily use of the line. Apart from this, the running of a full train from start to finish of the journey is more economical than the condition of most suburban traffic, in which the load begins to diminish at the first stop, and most of the trains have one-third or two-thirds of their seats empty for a considerable part of the journey. The rolling stock can easily be diverted to the lines where midday traffic is most intense. The capital cost of the permanent way itself would be immensely reduced if the routes were reserved in the regional town plan. Moreover, the means of transport are now so varied that one suitable to most kinds of load could be provided if there were effective co-operation between the town planning and the transport authorities; while the efficiency of the transport itself could be increased and the strain on the roads greatly reduced if all the various means now available were co-ordinated under one general direction.

The haphazard growth of our towns has encouraged haphazard thinking about them. The owner of a building site is naturally obsessed by the importance of securing the most intensive utilisation of it. When he has fully occupied existing buildings he will want to crowd it with others, and when these in turn are occupied he will seek to pile more storeys on the top. The town planner, surveying the territory as a whole, may take a very different view: he sees that it is often less costly to acquire a second site than to overcrowd the first; he realises that midst the scarcity of many things there is no want of

149

space, and that whatever the cause of congestion it is not due to lack of land.

Some truths seem too obvious to be readily credited; men are prone to try clever and complicated devices to attain the same end by a more devious route. Perhaps the nation is feeling specially poor, but, to produce more wealth or to waste less, seem too simple methods of enrichment to be popular. Oppressed as we are too with the miseries of overcrowding and housing shortage, how hesitatingly does the simple remedy of building plenty of good houses secure full recognition! Similarly, the towns being already unbearably congested, and the traffic in their streets in danger of being reduced to crawling pace by its excessive volume, the idea that congestion would best be relieved if we desisted from crowding or traffic most effectually be reduced by better distribution of people and buildings, is much too simple to be readily accepted. Indeed, many seem bent on piling more building on the top of that we have, and boring more subways or erecting more elevated tracks to pour their additional multitudes into the already swollen torrent in the streets.

To the town planner this looks like sheer madness: but perhaps there is something unusual in his make-up which predisposes him, with childlike innocence, to put more faith than some of his neighbours in the simple and the obvious. Or perchance, if an architect, there is something in his training or his practice which encourages this tendency. At least it is a fact that the Art of Design which it should be the purpose of his training to develop and his life work to practise consists largely in finding simple solutions for seemingly complex problems. When the designer cannot see the forest for the trees he is a lost soul! He must depend on his trained imagination to keep the forest as a whole ever clearly in his view while his mind is occupied threading its way through the obstructing trees and their distracting shadows. If he misses the one simple and direct path to unity, which when found will appear to all to have been quite obvious, he will usually have produced not a design at all, but a mere compilation.

I have ventured to draw from American cities a warning as to some things which we should avoid, and to use their experience as a guide for our future steps. Lest I should be thought to undervalue the marvellous civilising achievement which those cities represent, or to be lacking in appreciation for the genius which their architects have shown in handling the novel and complex problems in design which have been presented to them, I propose to show you a few examples of their recent buildings to illustrate the difference between a design and a compilation. Some of their lofty buildings soaring up many hundred feet into the air are as beautiful as they are impressive. And the same sense of unity and simple rightness is as evident in many of the buildings which do not derive impressiveness from their height. The Lincoln Memorial is a temple as worthy of the commemorating nation as the statue it contains is appropriate to the man whose memory is there lovingly enshrined. It is one of the most moving buildings I have seen. The architect, in spite of the distractions of log cabins, freed slaves, and the hundred other accessories that crowd around that picturesque life story, has gone straight for the main simple purpose; a great nation remembers its greatest son.

Men who have achieved within a few decades such culture, such a high level of design as these buildings display, when they turn that capacity upon the problems of town planning, as they are beginning to do, will, I am convinced, achieve equal success.

Beautiful as are many of the towers of New York when considered singly, there is yet lacking to me the sense of grouping between them which would spring from their forming parts of a greater design. Fine as individuals, they bear yet little relation or proportion to each other. I am inclined to compare a cluster of them with the three related towers of that older Lincoln which we prize.

However that may be; as architects we are trained to rely on orderly planning and proportional relation; and we naturally believe that they can be applied to towns; that the application of foresight and planning would result in the better distribution and relation to each other of industrial, commercial and residential areas, and could secure the more generous reservation of belts of open space to protect and define the different parts of the town, the wards, the suburbs, the dormitories or the satellite towns; that cities should extend not by fortuitous accretions around the circumference, but by the addition of definitely planned and defined suburbs or satellite towns, each made as self-contained as possible, depending on the main centre only for those functions which are by their nature centralised; that the position of suitable rapid transit lines to connect these parts to the centre and to each other could be laid down and reserved, and that congestion of street traffic could be prevented not only by the provision of adequate roads, but mainly by the proper localisation of the life of each district, and the saving of a large part of the useless carting and rushing about which now springs from so many people, buildings, and parts of the town being in the wrong places. We are convinced that congestion will be cured not by increasing the density of the crowd, but by transforming the crowd into an orderly queue. This at least is the alternative we offer to the policy of expansion upwards, being convinced that nothing can be gained by crowding.

9

Regional Planning
with Special Reference to
the Greater London Regional Plan

*A paper read before the Royal Institute of British Architects
on Monday, 6 January 1930.*

MANY will recall the fascination with which they first realised how the mysterious and beautiful form structure of crystallisation could be induced to spread through a formless solution. Some may remember how the molecules or atoms of a refractory mass might be stimulated by example; the introduction of a minute crystal of the substance being enough to rouse their traditional love of order; to cause the most active to 'set to partners,' these starting an enthusiasm for their appropriate movements which inevitably, if gradually, spread through the whole mass.

The introduction of the principle of planning into human affairs that have long been allowed to develop haphazard has a similar effect. Once the order of a plan is established over a certain area, the boundary, where order ends and disorder commences, forms a line of nonconformity, stimulating attempts to remove the irritation by spreading the order further and further. Within the short space over which the older generation of us can now look back, we have seen such a change in progress. We remember when buildings were generally considered in isolation. Then one or two examples of intelligent land planning and harmonious relations established between the buildings, as in Bedford Park, were dropped among us like the minute stimulating crystals. Thereafter incongruity between buildings and their surroundings was no longer accepted as inevitable; a sense of disorder and irritation was aroused. Those who felt the discomfort most keenly, sought to plan larger areas; and the order spread to more extensive sites, to whole villages, suburbs, and even new towns. Then came the sympathetic statesman, and in 1909 John Burns gave the power to local authorities to spread this order over those parts of their district "likely to be used for building purposes"; a phrase fairly liberally interpreted. The planning could, however, no more be limited by local government boundaries than by the acreage of a single site. Active authorities began to plan in their neighbour's ground; then they formed groups or regional committees to extend the area; these groups further combined and we have now reached the stage of Greater Regional Planning Committees; and the end is not yet. Across the channel we may see provincial planning; across the Atlantic State and even Inter-State Planning Commissioners are actively at work. To-day, another sympathetic statesman, twenty years after, presides in the place of John Burns over the same Department; Mr. Arthur Greenwood has just said that the term Town Planning Act, having served its purpose, is now out of date; and he has promised extended powers. But planning cannot stop even at the greater region. Already main traffic matters are passing from local to national control; a Commission is sitting to consider the question of National Parks, and planning may be expected ere long to carry its crystalline structure to the natural limits set by the sea shore to our island home!

If the beauty of my crystal order simile tends at this stage to be overshadowed by the apparent rigidity of the mass, I believe the very newest science would come to my rescue, and explain that so far from being rigid, the crystal structure merely defines limits within which the utmost activity of atoms takes place, and would even suggest that the individuals composing the atoms may enjoy something very like free will and initiative. It will be safer, however, to abandon an analogy becoming embarrassing to traditional ideas, and to explain at once that the extension of the principle of planning to wider areas in no sense promotes rigidity, checks initiative, or curtails real freedom. The substitution in the crowd before the booking office window of a queue for a crush, so far from destroying any real freedom, greatly facilitates the satisfaction of the wish of each to obtain a ticket.

The site or regional plan, like the queue, greatly adds to the sum of effective liberty by defining the limits and protecting the sphere within which each can move without being obstructed by others; and by bringing that sphere into appropriate relation with the many others with which each must have dealings. This general principle must be kept in mind, for it determines the legitimate limits of planning, as well as the proper relations between the several authorities who must undertake the work as its advantages spread to wider areas. If the site plan, having secured to the individual plot-holder space, prospect, and harmonious relations with the surrounding environment, needlessly restricts the initiative of the owner in detail of plan or design, then it has exceeded its proper function. In like manner the town plan, while securing harmony of surroundings and convenience of communications for each site, should leave plenty of scope for the exercise of freedom in site planning for which these larger advantages have afforded opportunities. If Regional Planning is to serve its proper purpose, that, too, must be made effective for solving the larger problems of distribution and intercommunication, without depriving the present Town Planning Authorities of the opportunity to plan their areas, or restricting their freedom to do so in accordance with local wishes, provided they respect the framework of the regional scheme.

One main reason which justifies the Minister in speaking of the Town Planning Act as growing out of date, is that it does not give reasonable opportunities for regional planning, or adequate facilities for site planning. At present Regional Committees must be content to give advice only, or they must take over from their constituent local authorities the complete making of their schemes. The first alternative is ineffective, and must remain so because regional proposals will often be as much outside the province as they are beyond the financial resources of the individual local authorities. The second unduly deprives the local authorities of their proper freedom to plan their own district, and throws on the regional authority a mass of detail planning not easily to be coped with. Regional Planning Schemes should be made effective, therefore, without depriving the local authorities within the region of their freedom to make Town Planning Schemes for their areas. These schemes should in turn leave ample opportunity for more detailed site plans to be made from time to time, either by the planning authority or by owners or groups of owners. These facilities to make development or redevelopment schemes will be specially needed in connection with the redevelopment of areas already built upon. The application of town planning to these areas is certainly essential to complete the substitution of planning for haphazard development.

A better example of the need for such planning could hardly be found than is furnished by the controversy about the Charing Cross Bridge. Every detailed aspect of the problem seems to have been discussed in isolation from the whole, the interest of the railway company, the navigation of the river, the connection of the approaches, the form of the bridge, and even the creation of terminal features; but no master plan for the district affected has been forthcoming. Such a plan alone could bring these and many other seemingly conflicting views and interests into some coherent relation and proportion to each other. The importance to the area affected, near the geographical centre of this great city, cannot easily be exaggerated. The district is one ripe for redevelopment. Only such a plan can authoritatively set at rest the serious doubt whether the scheme is really the first piece of a fine new garment, or merely another patch on the seat of an old one. Without some master plan for the great urban regions, it is impossible to view each problem as it arises in true perspective, or to see its proper relation to the whole.

The extension of planning to the greater region, while it implies less preoccupation with buildings, streets, and other details of development, and involves the consideration of many new factors, nevertheless calls for little change in the main principles of design. Our buildings must fulfil the needs of their occupants, and conform to the science of building construction. The art of architecture is conditioned by these necessities. Rapid changes in either the use or the science may have a disturbing influence on traditional forms of expression, as we are realising! For town and regional planning there is emerging also a science of urban and rural development to which good designs must conform. This science, still so little known, is being disturbed no less by rapid changes of use and knowledge.

In each sphere like principles of design must be followed. Imagination must be applied first to appreciate, and then to create, those special values, whether of use or of beauty, which arise from bringing the various parts into right relations and proportions one to the other. In this way is unity of design given to the larger whole. The principle applies to parts of a pattern traced on a flat background; to the grouping of walls, roofs and windows into a façade; to the disposition of buildings and openings around a civic centre, or to the laying down of a pattern for distributing urban development over the undulating background of hill and dale, field and forest, forming the region. The main purpose of the plan is to secure the best distribution of the dwellings, the work and the play places of the people. The method should be to lay out this distribution in a convenient pattern on a protected background of open land. Only in this way can a right relation or good proportion be maintained between the developed areas and the open land. Here another serious obstacle to proper regional planning must be recognised. For no such secure background as this method of design presupposes is in fact available! All land is potentially building land, and the poor planner has to fall back on scraps of background, in the shape of open spaces, such as he can see some hope of purchasing. He must perforce be content with these oases in a limitless desert of potential building sites!

Nothing is more essential for good regional planning than power to secure an adequate background of open land. So long as anybody may build anywhere, and no effective power to control the distribution of building development exists, the evils of sporadic building and ribbon development will continue, in spite of anything we and the Council for the Preservation of Rural England may say or do. Under Town Planning Schemes reasonable regulations can be made as to what class of building may be erected in each area, and as to the height and character of the buildings, without incurring liability for compensation. Any attempt, however, to determine where building may best be located, and where the background of open space should be preserved, involves a liability for compensation which no planning authority will face.

Regional planning in selecting the best areas for building development, and thus preventing sporadic building from spoiling the amenities of the land and entailing useless costs for services of all kinds, seeks to do for the lands of many owners that which any sane single owner would do in his own interests. The reservation of adequate background of open land, so far from diminishing the total value of the building increment, is likely to increase it. That the planning authority should be liable for compensation because the plan allocates where this increment may be realised, and where not, without diminishing its amount, is clearly unreasonable. The single owner will realise that by allocating building on certain lands and reserving others from such use, he will increase the value of the former and diminish that of the latter, but that on balance he loses nothing, and stands rather to gain by the added attractiveness and value of the estate, which his planning has produced. So also, when there are many owners, regional planning will not reduce the total value, but it may distribute differently the prospect of reaping building increment. This is a matter for adjustment between the owners who gain and those who lose by the new distribution. It is essential to good regional planning that this principle should be recognised and that practical means, fair alike to the owners and to the planning authorities, should be devised for giving effect to it. No doubt there are many other amendments to the Town Planning Act which would be very valuable; but to technical men seeking to apply the right principles of planning and design to the use of land and its development for building, those which have been referred to seem the most important. They are:—

1. Regional planning must be made effective without depriving the local planning authorities of the right to make schemes for their districts within the regional framework.

2. Greater facility must be given in the Local Planning Schemes and in Regional Schemes also, for securing good site planning as land becomes ripe, for development or redevelopment.

3. Planning schemes should be made applicable to all land, whether built upon or not.

4. The present powers of zoning areas for different classes of building should be extended to permit the reasonable allocation of areas for building development and the reservation of other areas from such use, without compensation from the planning authority, but with power to adjust between owners any gain or loss of building prospect resulting.

The preliminary study of the difficult task set before the Greater

London Regional Planning Committee by the Minister of Health shows that only on the basis of powers such as those sketched can the work be adequately accomplished. That Committee is composed of representatives of the City of London, of the County and County Borough Councils, and, indirectly, through the various Regional Committees, of the other local authorities within the area having town planning powers. The district is that of the London and Home Counties Traffic Advisory Committee; it contains 1,846 square miles, and is approximately represented by a circle 50 miles in diameter. The population approaches 9 millions; a number so vast that to provide for its natural increase and outward movement, involves annual developments equivalent in scale to a large town. The population of the County of London has been diminishing since the Census of 1901. Since then, the whole of its natural increase, due to excess of births over deaths, has been migrating outwards, plus the number representing the reduction. This population flowing outwards has mainly settled within the Greater London region; although in the decade preceding 1921 the whole of it was not retained there, and there was a balance of migration out of the Region amounting to about 35,000 annually. The estimates of the Census Authorities since 1921 show a turn of the tide in the outer region, and in addition to absorbing its own natural increase of about 56,000 per annum, Greater London has received on balance an immigration from outside of something like 10,000 annually. This change of flow is perhaps explained by the movement of industries into certain sections, to which attention was recently drawn by the Chief Factory Inspector. In spite of the good effected by Regional Planning Committees and Town Planning Schemes, and mainly owing to the want of power to locate development, this wide stream of population spreading over the Region, from the congested centre, and now also from outside, has settled haphazard, without any co-ordinating design. It has caused the outstanding example of sporadic building.

The rapid growth of motor transport removed the limitation previously set by the need to be within reasonable distance of a railway station. Any part of the Region is now accessible for those who drive a motor car; and patches of sporadic building are breaking out all over the Region, which damage the amenities over areas of land, out of all proportion to that which is actually used for building purposes (Fig. 38). Such development will also involve serious difficulty and expense in regard to the provision of sewerage and other services.

The outward movement itself is not the evil. On the contrary it must be encouraged, unless the congestion of traffic in the centre is to become still more intolerable. Nor does the area of land required to give generous accommodation for this population, raise a difficulty.

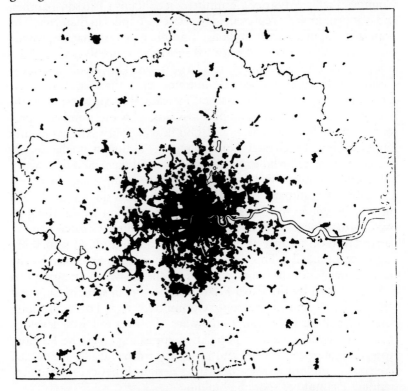

Fig. 38 The Greater London Region Showing the Main Developed Areas from "Regional Planning," 1930. Unwin's claim was that oversplash, rather than overspill, was occurring, that the lack of discipline and order in decentralization (suburbanism) was almost as great an evil as the congestion of the central city. The change-over from the railroad train to the motor car was making a bad situation worse.

If development were guided into reasonably self-contained nuclei (Fig. 39), forming attractive urban groups of different sizes, spaced out on an adequate background of open land, there would be ample space in the Region for any increase in population which may

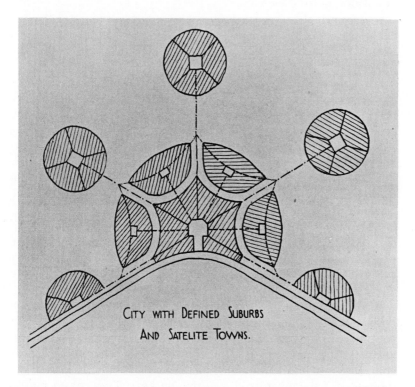

CITY WITH DEFINED SUBURBS
AND SATELITE TOWNS.

*Fig. 39   City with defined suburbs and satellite towns from "Regional Planning,"
1930. The hope was that with the application of crystallographic principles to
town planning, order would prevail and green spaces be left abundant despite the
automobile. This is the rudimentary diagram which eventually provided a justification for the new town cluster and greenbelt around London after World War II.
This outcome follows from the antidisorderly attitude of all the great urban reformers after 1850, including Howard, and the evolution of the microform of the
house into the superform of the regional plan, an escalation in scale which was at
the heart of urban problems from 1800 onwards.*

reasonably be expected, still leaving the greater part of the area as open land. Provision could be made in generous measure for playing fields, parks, pleasure grounds, wild country reserves, allotments, or aerodromes, and for the many other purposes for which an urban population needs open land.

The science of urban development on which planning for the distribution of this great population must be based, though far from complete, is too extensive to permit more than one or two items to be referred to by way of example.

For locating industry, determining factors are economical transportation, ready access to a sufficient supply of labour, and facility both for receiving raw materials and for distributing the finished products, whether they are consumed locally, in other parts of the country, or in foreign lands. The recent extensive development of industry in the area to the north-west of London is largely due to the coming of motor transport. From that district, while the London market remains easily accessible, practically the whole of the home market lying to the north and west can be reached without the delay of crossing London itself. Better bye-pass communications, such as the North Orbital Road, will probably tend to restore the balance of advantages in favour of the east-end and riverside sites for many types of industry. Other factors help to determine industrial areas, and much further study is needed in regard to them.

If productive industry may be regarded as the economic foundation of the social structure, commerce naturally follows. The expansion of commerce in the central area is the compelling force, supplementing a widespread desire on the part of many town dwellers to live in less congested and more rural surroundings; as such it is largely responsible for the great exodus to the outskirts. Two considerations dependent on a general plan may be mentioned, neither of which has received enough attention. The continued efficiency of a great organisation like the City of London requires that the most important operations, on which the welfare of the City and of the Empire depends, should be provided for in an area where they are not constantly hindered by crowds engaged in unimportant details, such as the purchase of gramaphone records, or the passing to and fro from the hatter to the tailor. Such confusion in and about the board room, the manager's office, or the quarters of the general staff, would not be tolerated in any other organisation.

The second consideration arising from the growing size of London's business centre is the reservation in immediate connection with that centre, of certain carefully selected and adequately protected residential areas, to accommodate comfortably the selected staffs which should be within call in connection with great enterprises. Planning of the built up areas can alone bring into play these principles of redistribution in reference to central functions. Large commercial and retail trade organisations are showing a tendency to maintain only the essential central functions in the congested areas; and to decentralise such departments as the storage of records, or the conduct of routine business, which can function as well or better outside. These tendencies deserve encouragement from the city planner.

The location of population moving to the outskirts can be arranged in accordance with like knowledge of their needs. Much is required in addition to the dwellings themselves. Shops from which to obtain their daily supplies, schools for the children, and places of amusement or worship are examples. The requirements of populations enjoying different standards of living, and the economical units for supplying them, are ascertainable within limits where judgment can reasonably be exercised. In rural districts about one shop for every 50 persons is the average proportion. In the large towns one for every 100 persons would be nearer, the average size of the shop being sufficiently larger to outbalance the increased degree to which town dwellers frequent shops. Average figures indicate that while one grocer's shop per 1,000 of the population may flourish, a furniture dealer may need 3,000. A musical instrument seller, or a dealer in sports articles, on the other hand, may hardly find sufficient customers among less than 10,000 or 15,000 people. Investigations in the New York Region have given an average figure of 50 feet of shop frontage for every 100 of the population. This would mean on the rural basis referred to above, 25 feet per shop, a remarkably reasonable figure, considering the difference between English rural and American urban conditions.

A number of such considerations suggests that units of from 4,000 to 6,000 people are sufficient to support a fair local shopping market for the supply of daily needs. Three such units, so combined that they could make use of one shopping centre, would be sufficient to support a very complete equipment of retail traders, and to add new possibilities for the maintenance of an adequate local recreation centre, institute, theatre or what not.

A reasonable proportion of open land for playing fields and pleasure grounds should be reserved in connection with each unit of urbanised population. To provide adequately for those who wish to play open-air games of all kinds in an urban area, there should be provided 7 acres of land for every 1,000 of the inhabitants. This would represent a need of from 28 acres for a 4,000 unit of population to 105 acres for a 15,000 unit. Experience further indicates that about one tenth of urbanised areas should be available for public open spaces for the enjoyment of open air life. As confirming this estimate, it is interesting to find that about double this proportionate area is already in use at Letchworth, where availability and ease of access are at their maximum. For the Greater London Region, this standard indicates a present need for about 200 square miles of open space and playing field.

As regards amenity, provided that the surrounding area can be protected from sporadic development, compact units of population of 4,000 to 6,000 people, and well designed groups of such units, can remain so nearly in touch with open country as to secure many of the advantages of country life. The selection of southern slopes which afford the best sites for such residential units would keep the northern slopes free to afford a rural prospect. Valleys and flat meadows less suitable for residential development, may afford good playing fields and belts of open land. If, however, belts of open space are required for the purpose of dividing or isolating residential units, even wide valley belts will be less effective than strips running along the ridges. The preservation of the sky line is more effective to secure rural outline to a view, than the preservation of much wider lands in the hollow.

That the better distribution of industry and population may result in the reduction of traffic congestion, the units of population should be made as self-contained as possible. While the best means of intercommunication for necessary movements is desirable, the congestion of this useful traffic by large volumes of that which is due to the bad placing or faulty relations of the different parts, is thoroughly harmful. The growth of motor transport which has extended the possible range for sporadic development, has also changed the character of traffic problems. To meet this, new types of road and methods of road planning are now needed. The outcry against ribbon development has laid stress on the destruction of amenity. Destruction of life, and obstruction of through traffic are equally serious results of unsuitable development on main road frontages. The motor car has rendered impossible the joint use of highways for traffic and for building frontage. Highways, in future, should be kept free from the obstruction and danger caused by numerous branch roads, or carriage drives, and by turning, standing, and crossing vehicles. The safety of the inhabitants must be provided for by arranging service roads and footpaths giving access from the dwellings to shopping centres, schools or other resorts, and reducing to a minimum the need to cross main highways. This principle is now so clear, that general effect should be given to it. No frontage development should be permitted on highways in future, without the provision of subsidiary service roads. As far as possible development should take place in compact units from which convenient access to the highway is arranged, but which are set back from it, and so planned that local intercommunication can take place with the minimum need for crossing the main highway. The North Orbital Road, which is likely to be one of the next to be put in hand, affords a good opportunity for demonstrating these principles, which are as essential for safety, economy, and efficiency, as they are for the preservation of amenity.

The few items referred to must suffice as examples only of a wide range of facts and relations forming the science of urban development. It is these and many similar considerations which must determine the main lines of distribution. The art of planning consists in bringing them all into such appropriate relations and good proportions that a coherent whole will be created, and will combine the many developments into a design on the background of open land, harmonising with the nature of the site. Thus there may be given at least the opportunity for a beautiful environment, out of which a good human life may grow.

"Housing and Town Planning Lectures at Columbia University"

The lectures of 1936–37 and 1938–39 appear to have been mimeographed. The former were bound and stapled in soft cover by the Sub-Committee on Research and Statistics, Central Housing Committee, Washington, D. C.

Lecture 1
October 1, 1936. The Nature of Man, His Life, in the Family and Society, afford the Best Basis for Good Housing and Planning.

ON opening this course of lectures, I would like to say first, that the course is intended primarily for the students, and will be directed to their requirements particularly. At the same time, the course is open to anybody who likes to come; and as this subject is one which at present is especially appealing to many from the humanitarian side, there is good reason for this. In the second place, I would like to ask your indulgence because I am called upon to fill the place of the late Henry Wright. He was cut off in the prime of life, on the threshold of a valuable career as teacher of subjects which he had studied and practiced for many years. He was my valued and respected friend, and I very greatly regret the loss we have suffered. You all have special cause to regret that loss. His career, gifts, thoroughness, and industry in pursuing the subject will be much missed. I am glad to think that my long association with Mr. Henry Wright's work, and the fact that for the last 25 years I have had close contact with people interested in housing over here, and have made frequent visits, will minimise but cannot remove the difficulties I face in this work.

There are many things which you as students have a right to expect in this school which I am not qualified to give you; and you will have to turn to Mr. Feiss and other members of the staff who have the intimate knowledge of your conditions which I can never have. Now, facing you young people, who yourselves are facing a new subject, Housing and Town Planning—housing the community as well as the individual family—and realising that some of the accepted views, those associated with planning particularly, may seem to run counter to your ideas of individual liberty, I have to ask myself wherein I can be of help to you.

For many of you those are new subjects; and I cannot stress too strongly at this time the importance of human psychology in studying the housing and planning of a community. From knowing man, his likes and dislikes, his habits, conventions and prejudices, we learn much that is important when considering the way he should be housed. In a study of the history of housing also we may trace the rise and fall of certain essentials of housing and planning. We may find what has proved successful and what has proved unsuccessful.

Compared with that of my youth, the world in which we live today is a changed place. Let me recall to you that in my young days a gloom rested on all economics and sociology. The Malthusian theory was then believed by most as gospel truth. This taught us that population would always tend to increase faster than subsistence; that there would never be enough of material goods to take care of the ever increasing population. A pessimistic idea indeed, and one which undermined progress of many kinds. Today we think more rationally; indeed, our present cause of worry in England is, lest there be a decrease in population.

We realise now that our main problem has become one of how to secure the effective distribution of the great amount of goods which we have learned to make, rather than that of how to create enough goods to go around.

After all, man's needs for a physical existence are few; and he is the most adaptable of all animals. Human beings have survived in the most adverse circumstances, and flourish in a great variety of conditions. We have Eskimos adapting themselves to a frigid climate; we have the natives of Africa living comfortably in their tropical environment. Men live in damp and in dry regions, in high and in low altitudes.

Consider also for a moment the main faculties of this animal man. He has dexterous hands to turn to many uses. He has the power of thinking and of deduction. He possesses emotions giving rise to strong likes, dislikes, loves, hates, and passions. Furthermore he has a retentive memory that enables him to remember not only facts but feelings and sensory impressions. Out of this ability there grows the power of association, which influences his prejudices and his convictions, and gives rise to many of his standards, values, and conventions.

This last ability of man is one which an architect should thoroughly understand; for differing customs, habits, and conventions determine various types of housing. A house must supply the proper atmosphere for the people who are to live in it. Equally, the plan of a community must provide the requisite satisfaction for the desires and purposes of the group of people to inhabit it.

This leads us naturally to consider tradition and the part it should play in modern architecture. The young man is apt to scoff at tradition; to want to throw aside much that has been done before and confine himself solely to what is new. The advantage of the approach of youth is that he comes to his problem with a fresh viewpoint and a mind open to experiment. The older architect, through this power of association of which I have spoken, has built up preconceived ideas and prejudices. He clings to the things which he learned to like early in his career. He, too often, has a mind closed to the new idea and the fresh viewpoint; but he has an advantage over the younger man in that he knows the value of tradition; he has had the opportunity to watch change; to note progress step by step; to learn the value of the good features in the old methods. We need both tendencies; the important matter is that there should be mutual understanding as to the limitations in both viewpoints.

To return to our discussion of man and his many abilities; finally he has imagination, the greatest gift of all. And this is really the chief faculty needed by any designer. It is the creative concept or imaginative quality in the design of a building, or site, or city, which differentiates the outstanding from the mediocre. I shall refer a good deal to this quality of imagination in a later lecture. Let me say here, before leaving the subject, that all designs should originate in the imagination, brooding on the problem to be dealt with, and controlled in the working of it out by full knowledge of facts and conditions.

Thus man has all these abilities or powers of body, mind, association, emotions, and imagination. But no two men are alike; the proportion of these abilities possessed will vary in each. It is this varying proportion possessed of these assets which makes up individuality. This is often confused with individualism, which represents really something quite different.

Man has always been a community forming animal, rather than an individualistic one. Again, do not confuse community with communistic. There is a parallel here, of course, but actually the two words as used today mean quite different things.

That community life is fundamental for man is proven by the earliest remains discovered. Long before evidence of advanced craftsmanship, we find relics of community life. This community forming habit exists in other animals: wolves, crows and beavers are examples. To find the most complete form of community life, however, we do not look to the higher mammals, but to insects. Insect communities are based on the most complex subjugation of individuality to community interests. An extreme example of this kind of subordination is found in one species where certain of these insects are hung up as living storage jars of food for the other insects to draw upon, so that there may always be easily digestible food for the community at large. So far as we know, in the insect world there is stagnation in the community, there being little or no change or progress in their ways of living together.

Modern community life among men is not like this. As a matter of fact, the tendency is to rush from change to change even more quickly than man can assimilate the new ways or learn the fresh lessons; for we, so far, have based our communities largely on taking advantage of the different endowments of men, on their individuality in fact.

I believe that man's greatest achievement is this ability to found his community structure on taking advantage of the differences in the abilities of various individuals. As a simple example of this: If a man had a secretary who remembered exactly the things which he remembered and forgot all the things which he forgot, she would be of little use to him. On the other hand, if he had a secretary who remembered all the little details which he had a habit of forgetting, but who forgot the things which he found easy to remember, then they would work with an efficiency much more than doubled, she filling in his deficiencies, and he filling in hers. Cooperation among men of different capacity is the secret of enhanced power and progress: it is limited only by their ability to understand each other's differences, and to appreciate their value.

In our complex modern society there are, unfortunately, many factors which are dangerous to this cooperation. The division of society into many classes is one of these, for this means many extremely different manners of living. In our slum dwellings, for instance, people live on such a different standard, the scale of values to them must be so totally different from that of people with adequate houses, that we can hardly expect them to realise cleanliness and decency as we know them. Put a whole family to live in one room, and another family in a six-roomed house; and then ask each to live as decently as the other, and you are asking an impossibility.

We must, if we are to expect full cooperation from all, find means to satisfy for all the whole nature of man. Our problem in housing is to remove those lines which divide one group of people from another, and thus to create in place of this diversity of standards, one common standard at least of cleanliness and decency. Our experience in England is very encouraging. We have proved that if the slum dwellers are given decent and adequate dwellings the majority of them will soon learn to adapt their lives to the improved conditions. As many as 90 per cent in some cases have made good. Considering that many of them have been slum dwellers all their lives, and that naturally the ne'er-do-wells gravitate to the slums, records of 80 to 90 per cent making good tenants of the new houses provided are as encouraging as they are remarkable.

Illustrations—the wigwam of the Laplanders may serve to illustrate my point that the actual physical needs of man are few. An early Schleswig dwelling may be seen in the open air museum in

Copenhagen: it is a good illustration of community life. Here everybody lived together in one room. The master and mistress, their children and servants, the farm hands, and also the animals. Everyone together shared this common life, each supplying some of the common needs.

An old English single-room dwelling affords another example (Fig. 40). In the early days of the Saxons, everyone of a large household lived in that one hall, servant and master ate, slept, and revelled together in the one room. The master had a separate table, but this was the only planning mark of division between master and servant.

There is a rather amusing picture in an old MS illustrating the feelings of the people left in the hall, when a separate retiring room called the solar, for master and mistress, was first introduced. This separate room for the head of the house was the first definite plan-

*Fig. 40   An Early English Hall, from the Columbia University Lectures, 1936.
A togetherness brought on by circumstances was always of interest to Unwin. He
felt people so concentrated would be bound to find a way of living together, a positive quality he also noted in the squalor of the slum.*

ning division to be established between a lord and his retainers in their condition of living.

The next stage came during the Elizabethan period of English history. Before this all dined together in one great hall, and revelled together. In the Elizabethan period, however, a new psychological factor entered into the way of living. At this time there occurred a revival of classical education; this resulted in new tastes and fancies, and thus a separate recreation room for the elite was introduced, often known as the long gallery (Fig. 41).

There were two types of origin for early English communities. There were the free men who by vote selected one of themselves for protector, and who worked under him out of choice. There was the other type of society where men were divided into two classes: semi-serfs under the control of the lord or chief who often represented a

Fig. 41   Long Gallery, Haddon Hall, Derbyshire, from the Columbia Lectures, 1936. This separation and extension of indoor space symbolized for Unwin the negative drawing apart of the aristocrat from his followers, the end of feudal inter-dependence. Parker and Unwin started their architectural career in the vicinity of Haddon Hall at Buxton.

race who had conquered them. The life was less different than might be expected in the two cases. The lord of the land, or the elected chief, divided it into common fields for cultivation and each of these into strips, and gave it out to the other men to farm; some strips were reserved in each area for the lord's benefit. There was a village nearby where the lord's manor house and the houses of the other cultivators were grouped on the land. So persistent was this system that even in 1820 there were still villages with those large common fields adjacent to them.

Long after the Elizabethan period, however, when people of different classes and station had ceased to associate closely with one another in the sense of living together under one roof, they still lived together in the villages, and shared much of the life of these communities. This condition sprang from the multitude of personal relationships which existed between these people, and formed ties to bind them together. The landlord and tenants, parson and his flock, tradesman and customers, master and servant, farmer and labourers, doctor and patients, all were in direct relation and shared common interests forming a network of community life.

Those linking relationships exist today and must be considered in planning. In fact, planning must be based upon those ties between various kinds of persons who live together, each dependent for something upon the other.

An early Indian village where the plan was based upon a rigid caste system affords a marked contrast. One area was devoted solely to persons of the highest caste, one area to the next, and so down the line to the untouchables.

In some instances English village or town communities sprang up near a body of water; others near crossroads; others under the protection of a castle. A view of Castle Combe shows in the distance, the castle, and in the foreground the common market place which all the people living in the community used (Fig. 42). Along the road or street were many different types of houses; the small ones of the poor, and the larger, handsomer types for the more affluent. Again you see people of different classes living closely together. Nor must we overlook the amazing beauty of this and many other such villages, the charming combination of architecture and landscape.

Fig. 42   Castle Combe, Wiltshire, from the Columbia Lectures, 1936. The lecturer wished to call attention to the variety in sizes of the houses in a medieval village and their ultimate dependence upon a singular and specialized building such as a castle or church.

Castle Combe market place formed a meeting place for the sale and exchange of local produce (Fig. 43). In time small villages grew into larger communities. As an instance of this we may take Orvieto in Italy which is situated on the top of an eminence having precipitous edges. No vehicles of any kind, until a very short time ago, could enter. There were no large industries, nothing to compare with what are known as modern methods of manufacture; yet 8,000 persons

Fig. 43   Castle Combe market place, from the Columbia Lectures, 1936. The positive and conscious informality of a market meeting place carried on in many of Unwin's designs.

lived here together sharing their interests and needs. The community was almost entirely self-supporting, yet created a finely built town.

One may note the market place and public buildings, how beautiful is the architecture, while the cathedral is one of the finest buildings in the world, with gorgeous carving and inlay work on the exterior, and inside some fine frescoes and paintings. This may remind us that merely satisfying the physical needs of man is not enough. The cultural side of life has always been important.

Certosa Di Pavia, the Monk's Garden, affords a glimpse of life devoted to the tending of other people's needs, the spiritual needs of man; the whole design expresses rest and peace in a strange degree.

Ancient Oxford was a city made up chiefly of colleges and churches (Fig. 44). A community, in short, devoted to the cultural pursuits of man.

An important consideration in housing and planning is the constant change in what is considered, from one generation to another, the minimum accommodation for decent living. Once again we see the link between housing and the human element. In an early English cottage, for example, we may find an old woman sitting comfortably in a small porch (Fig. 45). All through the history of English housing the cottage has been tied up with human life, human desires, needs, and habits as well as man's mere physical necessities.

Suddenly in the 19th century we seemed to break away from all this, to forget the human element. We went in for wholesale housing (Fig. 46)—houses built in quantity without regard for human life. The number of houses built seemed to be most important, not whether the people could live in them happily. Many an English slum has resulted from such building.

The worst slum conditions arise, however, when families, owing to pressure, come to be housed in one room. The results of life in these one room dwellings are much the same all over the world. Consider for a moment what life in one room for a whole family must be. Consider that there would be deaths, births, marriages, illness, everything going on in the one room where all must be. Imagine the mental and moral degradation that must result; the destruction of standards of decency; the bitterness and discontent that would be likely to arise from such conditions.

In the early industrial age, standards in family life and in housing deteriorated rather than progressed. What we are now trying to do in England is to get back to the cottage and garden type of housing. It seems to have proven itself, at least for England, the best manner of housing the poor. Such housing allows for the growth of individuality and imagination which are so vital to cooperation.

One of the first examples of a manufacturer's interest in the housing and welfare of his workers is found in the model town of Saltaire

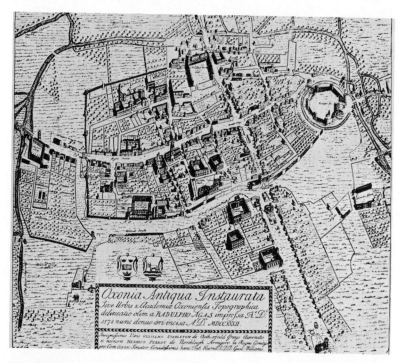

Fig. 44 Ancient Oxford, from the Columbia Lectures, 1936. Unwin spent his early youth in Oxford, where his father was a tutor. The quiet, cultivated, and thoughtful town rather than a hustling, industrial, or commercial city as an ideal environment for modern life was proposed in successive and different ways by Unwin. The quadrangular college was a persistent inspiration for joint dwellings designed by the architects, although William Morris also had a great effect on this.

Fig. 45 Porch of a small house, from the Columbia Lectures, 1936. The window bay, the inglenook, the porch, and balcony where the elderly could look out on the more active life of the community were indispensable and signified the constant wish to link up various spaces and generations.

(Fig. 47). It is interesting to note in this development that it was not considered necessary to give each group living in one of these cottages a garden of its own, but community gardens and places of recreation were supplied.

I have tried here to give you a brief glimpse of some of the housing problems of different periods of history in various countries so that you may better understand the problems of housing today. A picture of the Letchworth Estate shows what we are trying to do today in England to improve matters (Fig. 48). Each cottage in this town has its own little garden. These cottages are conveniently near the factories where the people work. There are also communal buildings and places of recreation; there is a swimming pool, a children's playground, etc. The Civic Centre is equipped with its shops, municipal building, post office, etc. (Fig. 49).

One of the architect's most important tasks is to think about and learn to envisage life in terms of human needs, desires, habits, feelings, etc. Upon this knowledge of man and human relationships is housing and community planning based. You do not need to be students of psychology, in the sense of knowing long words and new terms, inferiority complexes and the like, but only to the extent of understanding human nature. Through this understanding you will be able to better conditions. And here your faculty of imagination will be most useful.

Lecture 10

December 3, 1936. The Provision For Recreation.

AMONG the many provisions for recreation of various forms needed in town and site planning, the main ones for us to consider today are those for open air recreation of all kinds. They range from small tennis courts to children's playgrounds, to football and cricket fields, golf courses, and, in wider regional planning, the open air spaces given over to camping, hiking, boating, skating, etc. Open air recreation is of great importance at the present

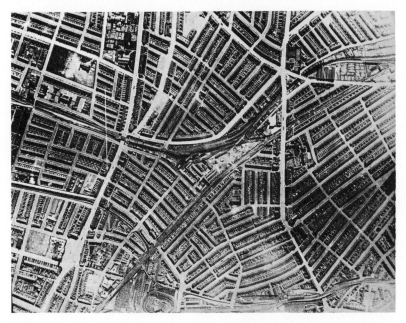

Fig. 46 South Shields, from the Columbia Lectures, 1936. The enormous quantity and the routine and impersonal quality of nineteenth-century industrial housing bothered the architect greatly.

Fig. 47 Plan of Saltaire (1850–1863), from the Columbia Lectures, 1936. Unwin knew the early industrial villages as well as the medieval and classical prototypes. The larger factory in the upper right required the smaller village. Salt consolidated six of his factories by this move from nearby Bradford. There had been no room for expanding them individually in the bigger city. The population of Saltaire was supposed to be 4,356. The tidiness and modesty of early model industrialism of the 1850's is as evident here as in the more famous London Crystal Palace by Paxton of 1851 in which Salt was greatly interested.

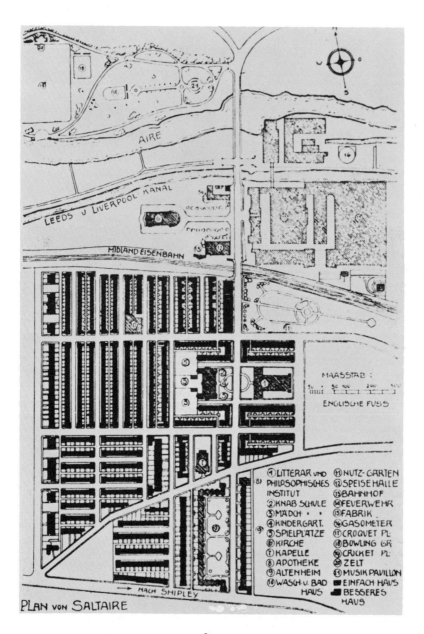

MAASSTAB :

ENGLISCHE FUSS

④LITTERAR UND ⑪NUTZ-GARTEN
8) PHILOSOPHISCHES ⑫SPEISE HALLE
INSTITUT ⑬BAHNHOF
②KNAB SCHULE ⑭FEUERWEHR
⑤MÄDCH · · ⑮FABRIK
④KINDERGART. ⑯GASOMETER
⑤SPIELPLATZE ⑰CROQUET PL
⑥KIRCHE ⑱BOWLING GR
⑦KAPELLE ⑲CRICKET PL
⑧APOTHEKE ⑳ZELT
⑨ALTENHEIM ㉑MUSIK PAVILLON
⑩WASCH U. BAD ■ EINFACH HAUS
HAUS ▬ BESSERES
HAUS

→ NACH SHIPLEY

PLAN VON SALTAIRE

SITE PLANNING at LETCHWORTH

Good Gardens, Allotments & Playing Greens. Inexpensive Roads.
Pleasant Surroundings.

Fig. 48 Pixmore Site Plan at Letchworth, from the Columbia Lectures, 1936. The characteristic Parker and Unwin motifs are just beginning to alter here as with the quad starting to become the cul-de-sac in several places and the uncertainty of street and corner setbacks. The secondary road meandering through the middle relates to their slightly earlier New Earswick settlement near York, but the dependence upon the free form superblock as the underlying, allover pattern marks it as a Letchworth layout. The superblock with a common allotment in the middle undoubtedly derives from Lord Leverhulme's model industrial village of Port Sunlight near Liverpool, which came mostly from the spirit of the 1890's.

time. There is a growing tendency in jobs today towards complete concentration on the one process being performed—extreme specialisation in other words. This necessitates the cultivation of recreational hobbies to balance the restrictions of the day's work; and the fact that the working day is becoming shorter and shorter, also means that more hours than ever before are now given over to leisure time interest. In fact, I think it is safe to say that we can expect recreation to play a larger and larger part in town and site planning. A greater proportion of work now being indoors, is another factor increasing the need for open air recreation.

The other important point is that we need to do something to counteract the present trend of thinking of recreation as consisting chiefly, either of playing cards and other more or less static games, or of flocking to see others play football and more active games. This is the most unsatisfactory form of recreation that exists. Persons who

Fig. 49 Leys Avenue Shopping Center, Letchworth, from the Columbia Lectures, 1936. Medieval flexibility of concept could to a degree accommodate contrasts in street style and scale.

go to watch a football game are not, of course, necessarily unfamiliar with the playing of the game. As a matter of fact, those who participate in some form of recreation usually enjoy watching the same game well played. Vast numbers, however, are content, or obliged to be satisfied, only to watch others play the games. This is very different from active participation in the playing. This flocking merely to look on is a bad habit which has grown up, and we must seek to break it by securing better opportunities for all to play the games themselves.

ILLUSTRATIONS

We have a good tradition of games in England. It is the usual thing there for the village to have a green or common. There is no lack of room there for young people to play the fashionable game of the moment. The village of Astbury with its church and village green adjacent, affords a typical view (Fig. 50). This is a small green, but the different classes can play together. It is perfectly true that on these commons the squire's son and the agricultural labourer's son do play together. We are trying to keep this attitude and conception of recreation alive in England, and to extend it. In the Hampstead Garden Suburb, for example, a village green was placed opposite the clubhouse.

Also in my country, we find much recreation in cultivating our individual gardens. In Pittsburgh I saw Chatham Village, which is one of the most interesting and attractive of American housing schemes. It is well carried out and very attractive; but I found that the whole of the land is kept up by the owners of the houses, and the cost of upkeep is covered in the rent, coming to about 50 cents a room per month. In our country, it works out the opposite way round in our housing schemes. Instead of the upkeep of our gardens costing money in extra rent, the upkeep yields money to the occupiers. Working-class gardens are mainly vegetable gardens, which more than pay their way. In other words, some revenue from the gardens would generally be secured. Carefully kept accounts show that this may often amount to about $2.00 per month. The difference between paying 50 cents a month per room for a garden, and making a garden yield produce worth from 50 cents to $2.00 per month in the value of its produce, is considerable, is it not?

In thinking of recreation we must think of all kinds of recreations; we must provide for the old people who want to sew or knit, or what not, perhaps by a seat in the porch (Fig. 45); we must think of little children who can't yet go up and down stairs, much less across roads alone; and we must think of the young men and women who need active games.

The front garden of a working-class house in England is mainly devoted to shrubs and flowers (Fig. 51); with a density of 12 cottages to the acre, there may, of course, be gardens both front and back of the house. We may contrast an interesting block of flats built by the London City Corporation, where there is nothing but a paved yard

Fig. 50   Astbury, Cheshire, from the Columbia Lectures, 1936. The village green shows up early in Parker and Unwin's ideal schemes (cf. Fig. 9) and certainly northern villages like Astbury had an influence on Port Sunlight. The implication was toward the ancient adult association which games on the green still reflected, when, as Unwin noted, "on these commons the squire's son and the agricultural labourer's son do play together." He declares that this was his chief reason for placing a village green opposite the clubhouse at Hampstead Garden Suburb.

where people can sit, or children play. This does not supply adequate recreation, or indeed, any reasonable open air facilities. Because a person lives in the city affords no valid reason to deprive him of the opportunity for any of the recreation which would be afforded him outside the city.

In certain countries one finds that good open space was provided, in or around the towns, in the interest of fortifications, etc. A picture of Vienna before the removal of the inner fortifications and the green belt surrounding them, shows how wide this space often was. This provided a good place for play and recreation. Later it was decided to remove the fortifications to a ring further outside the town, and al-

Fig. 51   English front gardens, from the Columbia Lectures of 1936. The need to protect flowers and shrubs from children and dogs was the cause of never yielding to the American "open front" system, perennially recommended by English reformers in order to unify the street picture.

though some open space around this area was kept, much of it was used for building, for sites for important imperial and town buildings, and the remainder chiefly for decorative open space. Vienna has been very enlightened, however, and progressive in its provision for recreation, having acquired an extensive ring of lands outside the city, and preserved them from building use.

To show the intensity of need for different types of recreation, a picture of the Rhine at Cologne may serve, with the crowds of people who flock to the banks for bathing. A line of boats is formed to guard against drownings, etc. The Central Promenade of Blackpool in Lancashire affords another example in England of the need to provide for the recreation of the masses of people in industrial districts. This is the closest thing we have to Coney Island. But this is not sufficiently near a great city for short day outings on an extensive scale. Provisions for rational recreation and games are not too good.

The intensity of desire for games in Chicago, and the neglect to provide space were such, that they had to clear built-up areas, such as that at Stanton Park, to make playgrounds (Figs. 52A, B). This, of course, is vastly more expensive than if space for playgrounds had been provided in the first place. In that case, there were roads and frontage all around the play yard; this is a costly way of planning open spaces. If an open space of five acres were surrounded by building plots of, say, 66 feet deep, the whole plot would equal 7.69 acres. You would have a road frontage of 776 yards; at 12 houses to the acre you could have 92 houses, which would allow 25 feet of road frontage for each house: at 10 to the acre there would be 77 houses giving 30 feet of road frontage per house. Each house could well carry the cost of the road work for 25 or 30 feet of frontage, and so the road would be paid for. If you planned the five-acre recreation ground with the road round it, the amount of road frontage would be 600 lineal yards; at $15.00 per lineal yard for half the road that would represent $9,000. If the land cost were $1,800 per acre, this would mean that you would be spending the cost of five more acres of open space just to have a road all round the first five acres. It is worth while to consider, whether for playing fields or other open spaces, any advantages from having roads all round are worth this cost; whether the extra size of play field might not be better value.

187

Figs. 52, A, B   Zabriskie Playground, Jersey City, N.J., and unknown village green, England, from the Columbia Lectures of 1936. Unwin made the point that crowded big cities brought crowded, expensive, and artificial playgrounds, surrounded by busy streets, in contrast to the old village greens.

In many English housing schemes a compromise has been arranged. Entrances with sufficient opening between the buildings to give a view of the open space are planned on each side. This involves road cost for short lengths, but very much less than all around; and yet you may produce very charming effects, and provide your open space more cheaply, or provide more of it.

Pageants and open air plays are examples of the kind of thing that people want to do. In New York, and in other congested towns, streets have been, and are closed, for certain hours to accommodate these and other forms of recreation—an expedient rendered necessary for want of proper planning. Pageants have proved a very popular entertainment in the Hampstead Garden Suburb, where suitable space was provided. Two or three times a year the inhabitants get up a pageant to celebrate some event, performing it in the open air. This brings together the different classes of people; the baker, the shoemaker; the business and professional folk, and the artists, all act in the pageant and get to know each other. When the suburb was built up, a place was set aside for such open air performances, where people can sit around in comfort and watch. That is the kind of provision one would like to make in all large housing schemes, as well as fields giving place for football, tennis, cricket, little children's games, etc.

You are doing in this country some very good work on these lines. Tibbets Brook Park, with its children's playground, its swimming pool and open air gymnasium, is a good example of which people take advantage, enjoying the opportunity for open air recreation. Another example is found in the big open air space, Bear Mountain Park, a large area where folk can wander about, camp, etc., equipped with place to park cars and for the steamers to land. These are, however, far from the people's homes: places to visit rather than to use constantly.

The Westchester County Park System is well known everywhere (Fig. 53). Much has been done to make the parkways ornamental. They serve the purposes both of speedy travel and aesthetic enjoyment. Rye Beach is another example of a complete recreation town. It shows certainly a very orderly arrangement. There is ample provision for the people to spend holidays, bathe and enjoy themselves in many ways. Jones Beach is a more recent example of good design applied to a recreation place.

189

The great highway of Ocean Beach Esplanade in San Francisco well illustrates the problem of the general habit of going to every place in automobiles in this country. There are so many cars packed together on the front that the view of the beach is ruined for the people on the broadwalk.

Radburn affords good examples of pleasant planning with open air spaces and park strips. The children can go out to play in these, and to walk along them to school, without going into the streets, which is a decided advantage. This consideration is getting more and more important because of the terrible number of motorcar accidents, both in your country and in mine.

Much in regard to planning is not easy to lay down in hard and fast rules and figures; it depends so largely on imagination. There is a plan of a small playground by Jens Jensen which is delightful: it indicates how much can be done in an imaginative way with those

Fig. 53   Bronx River Parkway, N.Y., from the Columbia Lectures, 1936. Such parkways around New York and Chicago led to their introduction into England at Wythenshawe by Barry Parker in the second half of the 1920's.

schemes. There we find the Council Rock, taken from Kipling's *Jungle Book*; the Old Folks Place is provided, camp fires, sand piles, etc. Children could make their own imaginative games in a place like that. The imagination of a child should be given full play; and you don't want to drill them into nothing but severely organised games. Space should be given over to children's imaginative play, and not all be devoted to formal, regimented forms of recreation. Children need simple things to play with; they will then invent their own games.

In England, planners think in terms of the minimum area requirement for recreation in towns as being about 7 acres per 1000 persons. The method by which that figure was reached is as follows: Each one-thousand persons contains about 500 persons between the ages of 10 and 40, the ages when people are most apt to want games of one kind or another: of that 500 persons, it may be assumed that 150 won't want organised games. There would be among that group, the disabled, people who don't like to play games, etc. Therefore, recreation ground for 350 out of each thousand persons ought to be allowed for. One acre serves about 50 players, on average; hence 350 players would call for 7 acres. This is by no means a generous provision; but it is far better than is available in the towns that have grown up without any plans making provision for recreation. In addition to this recreation space, it is considered that at least 1/10th of the area of a town is needed for ornamental parks, parkways, etc. This has no relation to population, but it is a proportion of the space, while the area given over to recreation is based purely on population.

Even in London, with its population of ten million, the recreation space on this basis could easily have been reserved with little addition to the size of the city.

Here are the figures: 55 square miles would be needed to give 7 acres per thousand for the population living inside the County of London, the area of which is 117 square miles; this space added would increase the radius by only 1.275 miles. If a like area for the remaining population were then added on the outside of the Metropolitan Police area, within which most of the ten million live, the two together, or 110 square miles, would only increase the radius of that area of London by 1.125 miles: so beneficial does the relation of diameter to area work!

It is most desirable to have the open space distributed at distances which are within easy reach for all the people, not all in rings. This, however, is a matter of planning, and would make no difference to the total size of a town.

Letchworth has given us a good opportunity for discovering how much playing space people would like to have. The town area and the land all round being owned by the Association, it has been evident that if the people were anxious to have one piece of land here for recreation purposes, it would not lessen the total building value, as the buildings which might have occupied that piece would go somewhere else. So at Letchworth it has been easy to give people as much playing space as they wanted. The figures of land used for recreation there are something like this: 106 acres of public open space for recreation, 162 acres additional space rented by clubs or schools for games. They have in use at Letchworth, therefore, considerably more than double the allowance of 7 acres to the 1000 persons. The total open space area represents 26 per cent of the town. The point that I wish to emphasise is, that, when the land is available at a reasonable cost owing to foresight and planning, the amount of open space which people like to have is much more than the 7 acres per 1000 persons aimed at for our towns. Further, I wish to emphasise that the size of a town is not seriously affected by the amount of open space, if it is sensibly planned. What we planners are aiming at is to revise present ideas in regard to open space. At present, we think of the whole site as a background of potential urban building; and we have to plan a meagre pattern of open spaces on this background of potential building land. Actually, the amount of building in relation to the amount of open space available is so small that this is foolish. The right way would be to plan a pattern of building areas on a background of open space. As a matter of fact, we are moving slowly towards this in England. The new town planning law enables the planning authority to say that outside the planned areas no buildings can be erected until a development plan is approved; that the need for new development must be shown; and if it would involve the public authority in excessive expenditure for drainage and services, then development may be prevented. This is the first step towards freedom to plan our real pattern of urban developments on a background of green spaces.

reserved for the growth of the several parts are all occupied. Thereafter, either there must be the confusion of parts expanding at the expense of other parts, or the town must expand by the addition of fresh
and complete units. If you will think of any other organisation that
expands, and that has a physical aspect like a town, for instance a
school, then you will understand what I mean. A school when it is
being expanded is not simply allowed to grow like Topsy, adding
more and more pupils to the already existing classes, and enlarging
the existing classrooms, but the whole plan under which the school
has been existing is recoordinated so that new classes and new classrooms and new facilities are added. Just so in a town, after a certain
point of extension, it is impossible simply to add to the town by adding patches of building around it, without causing confusion and congestion, and destroying the convenient relation of the parts. Sir
Ebenezer Howard first drew our attention to the possibility of providing for the growth of a city according to the unit plan; this was an
essential part of the Garden City idea.

ILLUSTRATIONS

Many very bad examples could be given from my country of unplanned town expansion. South Shields may serve (Fig. 46). Nowhere
here do you see any evidence of planning for the expansion which
has taken place. The different ownerships each have planned their
own piece of land to suit their own particular needs and tastes. They
have simply multiplied and crowded dwellings without any general
plan. In other cases, land has been used far outside the town for haphazard scattered developments which, though less congested, is in
other ways equally objectionable. This situation forced us in England
to adopt planning as a national and municipal matter. As a contrast,
the Hampstead Garden Suburb indicates some of the progress made
in London before the Town Planning Act was passed (Fig. 54A, B).
Here, 250 acres of land, subsequently extended to over 500 acres,
were laid out as a complete suburb, with all types of houses, schools,
communal centres, playgrounds, etc. You may see there some of the
possibilities there are for planning the expansion of cities. The com-
ponent parts of a suburb exist here and are grouped in an orderly

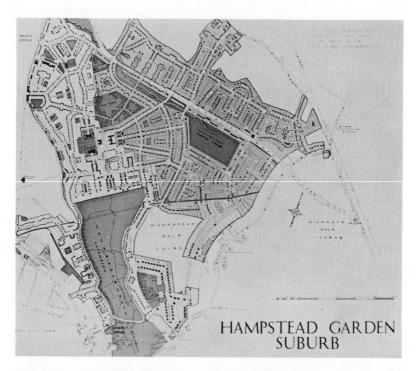

HAMPSTEAD GARDEN
SUBURB

Fig. 54, A, B   Hampstead Garden Suburb, from the Columbia Lectures, 1937. The cul-de-sac and the quad came into their own at Hampstead. The preservation of the tongue of extension of Hampstead Heath, in the lower part of the map, was the generating cause of Hampstead. The primary and secondary religious and pub- lic centers have fan motifs running out from them to the east and result from Un- win's desire to establish simultaneous open and closed spaces in his communities. The primary and secondary roads and gentle rises and curves follow a similar impulse.

way around the community centre, but they are not mixed up indiscriminately as results from unplanned growth.

Town Planning in England began with the Act of 1909 which dealt with the problem of regulating the expansion of towns. The schemes limited the density of dwellings varying usually from 4 to the acre to a maximum of 12 houses per acre. They also allocated certain areas for certain uses—residential, commercial, industrial, etc. This was the beginning of controlling the expansion of our cities. We are now trying to organise further the expansion of towns in more self-contained units. Many diagrams have been drawn showing such organised expansion for existing and imaginary towns to illustrate the method, and the many ways in which it can be adapted to varying conditions.

Another diagram illustrates ways of planning for the expansion of a town in greater detail. The large shops and big industries or other

197

full-grown institutions will not be needed at the beginning; but areas can be planned and reserved ready for them when the town grows sufficiently to warrant large stores, industries, residential neighbour-hoods, etc. In planning new towns and in planning for expanding towns, it is needful to provide for secondary shops, for small begin-nings, and for the larger ones which will be needed later. And you must plan for that future, when the more important commercial and industrial buildings will come in the centre of the town, when new and larger shops would grow up around the centre. Each of the resi-dential areas would develop correspondingly. The factory areas would grow. A time would come, however, when organisation of the growth into new and more or less self-contained units would be needed, then belts of open space, etc. may be planned to define each of the units, and to meet their needs for recreation. Having envisaged this, you would say to yourself: "This is about the largest size of central unit to provide for." If the town is to grow more than that, you would think: "Can we not adopt Howard's Satellite Unit Plan?" That, at least, is the conclusion which we town planners have reached as to the best form for towns; and it is one towards which we are al-ready working. The last revision of the English Town and Country Planning Act goes some way to enable progress on these lines to be made. By enabling the planning authorities to plan certain areas as open for and restricting other areas from immediate development, until such time as the owners can show that the town needs them also for extension, our town planning law enables us to begin to plan the form of the town. That is as far as we have gotten towards our aim, which is to plan the distribution of urban development on a back-ground of open area. The late Robert Whitten prepared a scheme for town expansion on these lines (Fig. 55), using a very low density zone as a means of reserving nearly open areas.

It is very interesting to find how often it seems that something fresh is not really new. In the port designed by Emperor Claudius at Ostia, we may see an example of a complete little satellite town develop-ment for Rome (Fig. 56).

In England, a definite advance in this direction has been made by the city of Manchester, in creating Wythenshawe, which is a self-contained suburb outside of Manchester (Fig. 57). The city bought up

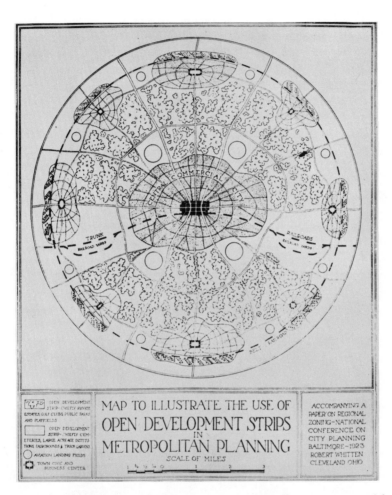

Fig. 55 Robert Whitten's Plan for green strips and satellite units, prepared for the American City Planning Conference of 1923 in Baltimore, from the Columbia Lectures of 1937. Radial-concentric planning was the basis of Unwin's later work on the London Regional Plan. This appears ultimately to have derived from Howard's idea that once the original garden city was filled to capacity, satellite units should be prepared around it (cf. Fig. 39). This is also the source of the broader disposition across the landscape of the new towns, although that is not now detectable in the relation of the new towns to London except in the vaguest manner.

199

Fig. 56   Ostia satellite city, the port of Rome, from the Columbia Lectures of 1937. Unwin liked to use classical as well as medieval precedents to demonstrate that his principles were endorsed by history. He also was intrigued by natural forms providing a logic for human settlement, as with the harbor here.

Fig. 57   Wythenshawe, satellite city outside Manchester, Barry Parker, from the
Columbia Lectures of 1937. This was the community most influenced by American
themes like the neighborhood unit and the separation of pedestrian paths and cars,
from Radburn, N.J. Through it runs Princess Parkway, the first in Britain and
also from the United States. The major scale and financing could only have been
possible in the latter 1920's, equating it somewhat with regional planning also developing in the United States during the 1920's.

201

the area, and also extended their city limits to include 5,776 acres. The city bought 3,710 of this, leaving 1,866 acres in private ownership. The population of the land at the time was 7,000. They planned a complete new unit for 25,000 houses and a population of 100,000. Here they are creating a satellite city to Manchester, with a new civic centre, areas for shops, and for light industries. There is also a large park of 250 acres. There a very definite unit is being carried out. I would just like to give you the densities aimed at. When there are completed 25,000 houses on 3,710 acres, which is the overall size and includes the sites for all buildings and everything, there will be $7\frac{3}{4}$ houses to the acre. In the working-peoples' residential section there are 12 houses to the acre: a mixed population has been aimed at here; they have already secured the development of a certain amount of land for well-to-do people.

There are some examples of such units in your country. One is called Greenbelt, and is just north of Washington, D. C. It is one of several built by the Resettlement Administration. They are planning for the present to build 1,000 dwellings, but the whole is laid out for 2,000 dwellings with a population of 8,000 persons. This land is adjacent to a large agricultural research establishment, and the planners of Greenbelt have looked to the future and realised that many of the workers in that establishment may want to live in Greenbelt. They have been amply justified here in planning for low density. The town itself sits on the crest of a hill that surrounds the end of a valley. In some of the schemes here, the maintenance of the open space is a considerable item in the rent. Where none of the garden land is cultivated by the occupants, the cost may be as much as 50 cents per room per month. In my country, the garden actually yields produce, sometimes as much as 50 cents per month. It puts money in his pocket, rather than taking it out, in exchange for his work in cultivating it. Compare that with having to increase rent to meet the upkeep. Here, of course, you are up against national habits and psychology. It is up to the people to decide what is best to do in this kind of situation—whether to cultivate the ground themselves, or pay in rent to have it done.

The city of Liverpool is now proposing to follow Manchester and to adopt the Satellite Unit Plan for part of their housing programme.

In Liverpool, they have already built 30,000 houses to house the lower income groups since the war. There are still 33,000 unsatisfied applicants for dwellings to be dealt with. The town council has committed itself to build 15,000 odd dwellings to house those to be moved from the slums, and they plan to build gradually 5,000 more houses to relieve the overcrowding revealed in the survey made in accordance with new law that has been passed. There are 680 acres in the new satellite site, and an aerodrome beyond the rectangular space. There are 5,000 houses to be built, with an overall density of 7.7 to the acre. The rents proposed are: $4.35 a month for the old folks' dwellings, which consist of living room, one bedroom or bed recess, kitchen and bath. The rent for the ordinary house, with living room, bathroom, kitchen and three bedrooms, will be $11.35 a month. It is interesting to note that they have also planned for some more expensive types of houses with an extra sitting room, which will rent for from $19.50 to $32.00 a month. They are trying to mix the people of various classes and incomes to a certain extent. They have planned a freeway all around the town, with no through traffic going through the town. There are school sites, a centre for the communal buildings, etc., and a little riverside resort nearby. I show you this just to emphasise the extent planners are beginning to think in terms of satellite units.

A few examples will indicate how much there is of historical background to city planning. Turin has been planned since Roman times. They adopted the checkerboard pattern (Fig. 58). The extent of fortifications shown on an early plan is surprising. When the town was extended, they planned a diagonal street leading to a bridge over the river: the street opened out into a long square at the bridge-head affording a good view into the town in one direction, and a view the other way showing the temple building at the end of the bridge, and a prospect of the hills beyond very attractive.

New York City adopted a similar checkerboard pattern, with, however, blocks of a different shape (Fig. 59). Today the two towns show the difference that New York expands to a large extent vertically, instead of horizontally as at Turin.

State Street in Chicago, Illinois, on a busy day illustrates that building upwards makes for traffic congestion and crowded streets, public conveyances, etc. (Fig. 60). The Paris sky-line affords a noticeable contrast to New York. It is low and uniform except for a few church towers here and there.

Planning has not always been as completely conscious as it is today; an old plan of Oxford shows this (Fig. 44). There was an extension plan in the early 18th century. The conscious and semi-conscious planning produced in the High Street one of the most beautiful streets in the world, because the building pattern has been planned along it so that it shows particularly well the great beauties of a curved road, which gives a changed view to any-one walking up the street, and displays in nearby front elevation, building after building on the concave side.

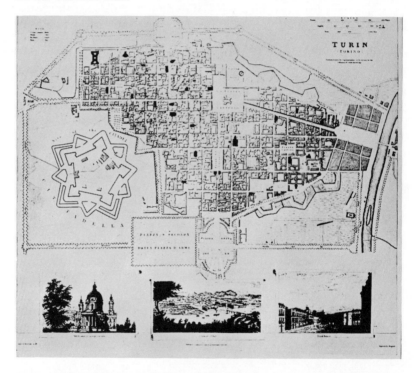

Fig. 58 Plan of Turin, Italy, from the Columbia Lectures of 1937. The orderliness of the Roman checkerboard plan attracted Unwin although he had little faith in it for modern traffic.

Bath shows some interesting planning of the 18th century (Fig. 61A, B). They believed in closely building up the street frontage, but there was plenty of room at the back. There were not more than 5 to 6 houses to the acre in many of the crescents and terraces, although they presented continuous row fronts to the street. This is true also of the circus with its garden and trees in the centre and the 18th century architecture.

Copenhagen affords some good examples of city planning providing for easy access to ships in the harbour; easy access in roads to and from the town; but as well as planning for convenience, they planned for beauty. That is what the good planner does. He does not sacrifice

Fig. 59   Midtown New York City, from the Columbia Lectures of 1937. The vertical expansion of Manhattan buildings on top of the traffic further invalidated the block scheme in Unwin's mind.

205

Fig. 60   Chicago Street, from the Columbia Lectures of 1937. Unwin believed that the verticality of the skyscraper overcrowds the streets as well as making them dark and windy. Larger and taller solids spoiled the voids.

beauty to comfort, or comfort to beauty. In planning a town he must have these two elements in mind, working at them together all the time. He must be able to picture the people going about their daily lives, and think all the time how this life can be provided for so that the city may be both pleasant and convenient to live in.

Lecture 14
January 21, 1937. Regional and State Planning.

ALL planning must be largely a cooperative activity. The number of basic spheres of knowledge upon which good planning must be founded is so great that no one person can acquire more than a fraction of them; and it is clear that the wider the range of the planning the more must this become true. It is indeed true enough in regard to city planning, but when to the city is added the whole of a region, and to that the whole of a state or nation, it is clear that planning must be based on contributions from many experts. One may mention particularly the spheres associated with the architect, the landscape architect, engineers of various branches, geographers, geologists, economists and sociologists, and even psychologists; for, after all, it is the behaviour of human beings in response to certain influences, and the effect on human beings of certain conditions, upon which alone good planning can be based. Nevertheless, in spite of this, and indeed because of this wide extent of contributions, there must be some one brain to conceive the new order of relations and the new plan in which they should be expressed and realised; for without this conception, any planning must be of the nature of repairing that which is, or adding to it patches of what is fresh.

The word planning is used to cover a wide sphere of activity in which the importance must shift from the visual conception, towards the known or reasoned mental conception, as the range dealt with passes from site planning through suburban, city, and regional planning, to state or national planning.

We have still to find the best methods for training men whose par-

207

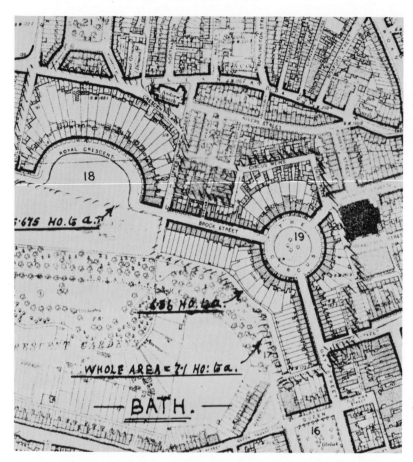

Fig. 61, A, B   Bath, England, of the eighteenth century, from the Columbia Lectures of 1937. The building up to the street was noted by Unwin but he qualified it by indicating the gardens in back and the green of the circus, crescents, and terraces. Buxton had similar resort housing amidst which he began his practice. The British architect of his generation was bound to be multiexperienced, and hence multisolutional, in his approach.

208

ticular function it shall be to sum up the contributions of the various experts, and to embody them in a coherent new plan based on a visualised mental conception. This is work analogous to that of a designer; and it seems clear that an important part of the training should consist in practising the formation of these conceptions of new relations, and of plans and arrangements of them; and as regards the physical aspect of planning, it is essential to practise such a clear mental visualisation of them that they can be expressed in the form of plans on paper. Where planning consists mainly in the formation of new economic or social policy, the visualisation is a much less important element, and indeed, may be absent. The wider the area to be covered, the more extensive becomes the field in which a reliable basis of fact must be accumulated on which alone any sound design can be based. One of the equipments of the planner must consist in an appreciation of the kinds of facts which will be valuable to him for the purpose of planning, and the power to ignore or avoid being obsessed by other kinds of facts which, although they may be of the utmost value for other purposes, are not such as can materially affect his work.

In regard to population; for example, the census returns may contain a whole volume of information, but may easily omit, and often do, two of the items most important to the planner; namely, the proportion of increase or decrease in local population which is attributable to migration, in or out of the area; and the number of family units, whether they are increasing more rapidly than the population, or not. As an example of the importance of the first of these may be mentioned that in the decade 1911–21, over 300,000 migrated out of London, not merely from the county of London to the outskirts, but right out of Greater London; whereas in the decade 1921–31, while the migration from the central area of London continued much as before, the whole of the emigration from central London settled during this decade within Greater London, and in addition to these, over 400,000 migrated from outside Greater London and settled within that area; so that while the county of London declined in population by nearly 300,000, the outer area acquired by migration, apart from the natural increase, something like 700,000 in the same decade. The importance of knowing the increase or decrease in family units arises from the fact that the need for dwellings depends on the number of families, rather than the number of people; and in England during the last intercensus decade, while the population only increased 5 per cent, the number of families increased by about 17 per cent; indeed, this element was the main cause of the great difficulty which England had after the war in overtaking the shortage of dwellings, and it was the chief reason why they have needed to build 3,000,000 dwellings since the end of the war.

Not only is it important to judge which facts will be useful, but it is important to learn how to represent these graphically, so that their incidence and effect may be apprehended quickly by the eye; and that the effect of the coincidence of two or more circumstances in certain localities may equally be located quickly by the eye. When representing statistics graphically, it is important that any graduation in quality should be clearly shown by the graduations in the intensity of shading, whether by hatching or by depth of colour; whereas any distinction in kind should be told by a clear difference in the character of hatching or in the colour used. A good example of the need for this is afforded by a most valuable map showing the intensity of agricultural use and the quality of the land for cultivation in the state of New York, where the method of indicating built-up land can hardly be distinguished from that used for one of the grades of quality; whereas a different method of shading was needed rather than one of a clear graduation, which should be used to show the relative quality.

The word region as applied to planning is generally used as indicating an area within which certain natural factors, particularly of a physical character, indicate the distribution that any planning should consider and be based upon for the whole of the region. Such physical characteristic, for example, is afforded by a large river valley, where the preservation from flood, the use of the water for power purposes, the navigation of the river and the distribution of cultivation and afforestation should be considered in relation to the whole valley. The area within which coal or other minerals can be found and are likely to be worked, may also become the basis of a region. The distribution of population in the neighbourhood of a large town may be another indication. For example, in London, the London County Council area of 117 square miles now contains only about 46 per cent of the 10,000,000 population of Greater London; the other 54 per cent is outside the jurisdiction of the Central London Government, and is included in more than 100 local governing areas. Clearly, therefore, no consistent planning for London could be undertaken without treating the whole of the area over which London has expanded as one region for planning purposes. While regions, therefore, do not coincide with areas of local or National Government administration, these latter areas must be taken note of and their importance may at times overtop even that of natural regional areas.

It would be very convenient in Europe, for example, if planners could sometimes ignore the national boundaries, in order to plan according to what might be much more natural physical regions; but the difficulties involved might very easily be greater than those of planning a natural region in two or more sections. Where the national or state boundary is one which for political or economic reasons it is difficult to overpass, state or national planning must be accepted as the unit, and is naturally concerned with the main features of the distribution of population both rural and urban, the development or conservation of national resources, the promotion of convenient means of intercommunication or distribution, the preservation of navigable conditions in rivers, the protection of the valleys from flood, and other similar large scale matters. Examples of large scale planning are for example; the electric grid which now distributes electricity throughout England and Wales, and the system of main highways in England which is being taken over by the Central Government from the County authorities who were formerly responsible for it. The Tennessee Valley scheme in this country is another good example, where navigation, flood protection are needed. The creation and distribution of electric power arise from these activities, and the necessity to prevent soil erosion and the redistribution of much of the population have led to one of the most interesting planning schemes on a national scale now going on.

In England, we have had an interesting regional distribution of architecture which may usefully form an example of regionalism on the aesthetic side. Owing to the fact that nearly all the main geological strata pass diagonally across our small country, and that the country was developed fairly evenly all over at a time when transportation was expensive, there have developed in the several geological regions, styles of architecture, particularly in regard to domestic buildings, based upon the most effective and attractive use of the building materials which were available in each region. In some cases, granite and slate were available; in others, a soft easily-worked limestone lent itself to an attractive stone building. In many parts this stone could be split into thin sheets very like slates so that the buildings could be roofed with a like material. This has given rise to the very attractive Cotswold building which characterises a band of villages stretching diagonally over a good part of England. In other districts, clay which could readily be burnt into roof tiles or bricks has dictated the style of building. In others, wood was the most plentiful building material, and we have houses built with a framing of wood filled in with plaster or wattle and daub, resulting in what have been called our "black and white" buildings, some of which were of great elaboration and beauty. In these cases in some districts thatch was the most readily available roofing material. It is indeed a matter of great interest, and of some surprise to those living in modern conditions, to see the high degree of quality and beauty which our forefathers were able to attain in buildings so admirably developed from, and adapted to the particular local materials which were most ready to their hands. They indicate an appreciation of quality rather than quantity which has been very absent from our civilisation during the last century.

May we not venture to hope that the conditions which have been particularly evident during our recent period of depression indicate that we are reaching the limit of the time when the main emphasis has rested on the quantity of goods which could be produced, and that we are approaching a time when we may be able to take quantity for granted, and again lay more emphasis and devote more time and labour to the securing once more of a much higher average of quality, both in the design and the character of all that we build or make.

I I

Land Values in Relation to Planning and Housing in the United States

URING the nineteenth century, conditions in the United States were so exceptional that they tended to create a conception of land values that was more fictitious than real. In a relatively new and unoccupied country, where rapid growth of population is taking place both by natural increase and by immigration and where industrial and commercial development is on an extensive scale, the influence of such forces tends to be associated too directly with the value of land, giving it an undue appearance of reality. This may lead to very serious mistakes when circumstances change. Land policies and methods of taxation, which may have had some justification when capital values of extensive areas of fortunately situated land were expected to increase annually in greater amounts than the incomes yielded, may become quite unsuitable when conditions are reversed, and the annual income (if there is any) may surpass any reasonable expectation of yearly capital appreciation. Such change of

The Journal of Land & Public Utility Economics, February, 1941 (vol. xvii, no.1). *Editorial Note.*This manuscript is the last work from the pen of the late Sir Raymond Unwin, the eminent British city planner. It has been made available to the *Journal* by Lady Unwin through Mr. Harold Buttenheim, Editor of the *American City,* Mr. Lawrence Orton of the New York City Planning Commission, and Professor Carl Feiss of the School of Architecture of Columbia University. With the permission of Lady Unwin, the manuscript has been edited slightly, primarily for purposes of clarification. Since unfortunately his source material is not available, the footnotes are entirely editorial additions, designed to aid the reader by indicating some of the probable sources of the data used by Sir Raymond. The editors particularly wish to thank Mr. Morris Hirsh for his assistance in checking computations and gathering additional figures. The advice and counsel of Mr. Walter H. Blucher, Executive Director of the American Society of Planning Officials, in the editorial revision are also gratefully acknowledged.

conditions has marked the recent years of the twentieth century, in which the cessation of increase in population through immigration and a rapid diminution in the rate of natural increase have taken place.

So long as the supply of butter is ample, each possessor of a slice of bread feels fairly sure of his share, and is not too much concerned with the thickness which his neighbor spreads on his slice. When, however, the supply runs short, all are interested in a fairly even distribution; if too much is spread on one man's slice, other slices will get none. That is exactly the position in regard to land value today. The total in sight is becoming more limited; and if too much is spread on a few plots of land, many other plots will inevitably be deprived of a share. This relative scarcity in the supply of value has therefore given fresh importance to the relation of density of building to concentration of value, and the extent to which high density tends to locate the total available on a few favored plots, at the expense of the general body of plot owners.

One or two examples will illustrate the situation. The first may be taken from Chicago, where records of the change of use and expansion of areas for different uses have been kept since 1923, when the complete zoning ordinance went into force. The population of the central area of Chicago has been diminishing for many years. The Census of 1930 revealed an area of nearly 50 square miles[1] over which such decrease had occurred. The estimated population, based on a careful survey made in 1936, showed this area to have increased greatly.[2] Of this central area, 44 square miles are now classed as definitely blighted,[3] and they are entailing a huge loss to the city. The

---

[1] Cited by Hugh E. Young of the Chicago Plan Commission in "Need for and Some Practical Method of Rezoning Urban Areas," a paper presented at the meeting of the City Planning Division, American Society of Civil Engineers, January 21, 1937 (mimeo.), Map 106. This map, however, shows the area of population decrease between 1920 and 1930 to be somewhat smaller than the 51 square miles referred to in footnote 3 below.

[2] This was true even in 1934 (Young, *op. cit.*, Map 107).

[3] "... in Chicago, ... we have a blighted district. ... It is the back yard of our lake front development. ... This [back yard] comprises a total area of fifty-one square miles, of which forty-four square miles are blighted territory." (Young, *op. cit.*, p. 11.)

total developed area of the city is 157.77 square miles,[4] and of the sub-urbs outside which constitute an integral part of the city geographi-cally, 76.50 square miles,[5] making a total of 234.27 square miles.

If the area occupied by commercial buildings in the city itself in 1923 be compared with the total area so occupied in city and suburbs in 1936, the result is an increase of 3.74 square miles in the 13 years, or .3 square mile per year.[6] If this total rate of growth could all in future be concentrated on the central area, it would take 146 years of such growth to redeem the 44 square miles of blighted area with commercial use. Now it is commercial use alone which yields the very high land values in central areas. If the actual increase in com-mercially used land within the city limits only had been taken, the figure would have been less than .2 of a square mile during the whole 13 years and the period required to cover the 44 square miles would exceed 1,500 years!

In view of the rapid rate at which the present value of a deferred realization of increment diminishes as the period is extended, what would the expectation of increment from commercial use over this blighted area be worth today, even if the whole of the future com-mercial development of the larger area could be located within it? Obviously, the prospect over three-fourths of the area has no present value.

How then would the picture look if residential use were adopted? In recent years the increase of population in Chicago has been slight; but from 1911 to 1930 the increase averaged approximately 60,000 per annum, requiring about 15,000 dwelling units. On the assumption that recent decentralizing trends could be reversed, the rate of in-crease recovered, and the whole concentrated in the blighted area, then the number of years required to realize value from residential use over the whole 44 square miles of so-called blighted area would obviously depend on the density adopted. If 100 families to the acre were copied from some New York schemes, 187 years would be re-

---

[4] That is, in 1936 within the city limits (Young, *op. cit.,* p. 9).

[5] Young, *op. cit.,* p. 9 refers to this as the "developed *residential* [italics supplied] areas beyond the city limits" in 1936. The suburbs included are those "that are in-tegrally a part of Chicago even though located outside the corporate limits."

[6] Young, *op. cit.,* Drawing No. 101.

quired to fill the 44 square miles of blighted area when population was increasing at the rate of 60,000 and dwelling units at the rate of 15,000 per annum. Lesser densities would, of course, shorten the period as follows:

Density per Acre	Absorption Period
50 families	93.5 years
25 families	46.7 years
10 families	18.7 years

If the highest density were adopted, the owners of the last part of the area to be covered would have to wait 187 years before any actual increment accruing from building would be received from their land. If the lowest density were adopted, they would all realize it within 18.7 years. This is one very important fact which land owners do well to consider, as would also the citizens of American towns having blighted areas, for whom the speed at which they can be redeemed is important. The question of the relative value per family which different densities would yield will be considered in connection with the situation in New York.

Meantime the effect of density in relation to commercial buildings may be noted. Though not so simple to calculate, this is equally decisive in fixing the period required to bring increment value to the whole of an area. An effective demand for a certain floor space for office, warehouse, and store purposes will occupy less and less land area in proportion as the business premises are piled in stories, one above the other, instead of being placed side by side. If 40 stories are adopted in place of 4, for example, approximately 1/10 only of the area of land will benefit by realization of increment. The general adoption of higher buildings, coinciding with the diminishing rate of general expansion, must undoubtedly share responsibility for the prevalence of blighted areas around the business centers of many American towns. But for that increase in height, the commercial areas would have expanded more rapidly, and more nearly kept pace with the flight of population from the congested centers to more commodious sites on the outskirts.

If the significance of this change in conditions is to be understood, the nature of land values must be recalled. Land is valued for two main classes of use: first, for the production of useful or enjoyable produce, whether food, game, raw materials, or precious metals; second, as affording sites for dwellings, industries, and commercial or social activities generally. The value in both classes consists in what folk are willing to pay for the privilege of using the land. Thus human psychology plays a large part in determining the extent of value which each kind of use may yield. There are, however, more tangible factors which may limit the value. In the first class, a limit is set by the extent of produce which any land will yield over and above the costs of production, including maintenance of the producers. This class of value attaching mainly to rural land will not much affect the present inquiry, except as fixing an approximate datum line of value per acre from which increased value for other purposes can be reckoned. Values in the second class attach mainly to urban land and are usually far higher than those in the first class. These values depend on the extent of population and of the activities, on the importance of being near to the center of them, and on the possible profit to be made by occupying the more favorably placed sites in preference to others. Here also human psychology plays an important part; but, as in the case of rural land, certain more tangible factors are fixing limits which must here be considered.

Before dealing with them, however, the important fact must first be emphasized that in both classes the real values only exist if, and so long as, the land is used, and the buildings on it are occupied for the respective purposes which create those values. Where land is not used or where buildings are not occupied, no actual value is being created, and no real land value exists. There will, of course, be a hope of future value in the heart of the owner; there may even be an expectation of such value which seems plausible to his mind; but until realized by actual occupation and use, both values are speculative, not real. The hopes or expectations of the owners may indeed be shared more or less by others, and a market for the land based upon them may arise. This, however, does not alter the fact that no real value exists; that what is sold and bought in such market is merely the chance to benefit by a hoped-for value, if it is ever realized. The value is of the same nature as the increase in salary which a clerk hopes to receive next year, and on which he may raise a loan if he can find anyone who fully shares his optimism.

This aspect of values needs to be stressed, because the very rapid development of population and urban centers during the last century conferred an unreal appearance of actuality on such speculative values. By constantly enlarging the limits of possible realization, moreover, such rapid progress tended to hide the existence of these limits; and where the increment in speculative capital value approached or exceeded annually the income realizable from use, a tendency was created to prize the unreal hope or expectation more highly than the real and realized value. These tendencies have been carried over into the present time, when conditions as to population have become nearly stable; when the increase both in total and in urban population has become both a small and a diminishing factor. No longer is there any promise of unmeasured expansion; indeed, both the area over which building value is likely to extend and the total amount of increment which there is now any real justification to expect have been very drastically limited by the change.

Conditions in New York may well be examined as a second example of the character of land values. Thanks to the survey made by the Mayor's Committee on City Planning,[7] information on a number of aspects of the problem of land values is available, especially as regards the residential use of land.

If the total of dwelling units for New York in 1939 is given as 1,890,618[8] and the population as 7,380,259,[9] we get one dwelling for each 3.9 inhabitants. From the rental statistics it would seem that the average rent per family on Manhattan is about $355.62 per annum, whereas for the whole of New York it is $442.80.[10] This difference arises from the much larger proportion of rents between $30 and $60 per month in New York and of those under $20 per month on Man-

---

[7] *Progress Report,* Mayor's Committee on City Planning in Cooperation with the Works Progress Administration, New York City, June, 1936.

[8] *Report,* State Superintendent of Housing, Albany, N. Y., January, 1940, p. 30.

[9] U. S. Census of 1940.

[10] The source of these data on average rents for Manhattan and New York has not been discovered.

hattan.[11] What precise proportion of these average rents may fairly be taken as representing ground rent must be conjecture; but if $\frac{1}{5}$ be taken as the proportion for New York as a whole, this gives $88.56 which would represent about $\frac{1}{4}$ of the Manhattan rents. Use of this figure of $88.56 as a rough approximation together with the number of dwellings given (1,890,618) would yield a total annual ground rent of $167,319,693. If this be capitalized at 4% on the basis of 25-years' purchase, the capital value would be $4,068,513,150, or 79 cents per square foot over the gross area.[12]

The land of New York is assessed for taxation at $7,076,271,087,[13] which is $2,893,278,762 above the figure reached for residential land,[14] an amount which may not unreasonably be taken to represent the assessment for the much smaller area of relatively more highly priced land devoted to commercial and other non-residential uses. If so, it would show a corresponding average of $3.28 per square foot for such uses. No doubt detailed examination of the data on which these broad figures are based would yield more exact results. These approximations, however, will suffice to indicate that the total available land value for an average family is ascertainable, and consequently the total fresh value which there is sound reason to expect will be yielded by an increase in population. The areas of land, used and vacant, in New York as a whole, and in Manhattan, are as follows:[15]

---

[11] ". . . predominant rents in six out of every ten blocks of the city were between $30 and $60 per family per month. . . . Only 8.7 per cent of the people pay less than $19 rent, and even fewer pay more than $60." (*Progress Report, op. cit.,* p. 40.)

"Here [Manhattan] in the heart of the city, we find 21 per cent paying under $19, and nearly 19 per cent able to afford over $60." (*Ibid.*)

[12] These figures are very close to an estimate, based upon data available in January, 1941 from the 1940 Census, which shows a capital value of $4,182,992,325 and a value per square foot of 81 cents which is derived by dividing the 185.75 square miles of residential area (see above) into the total capital value.

[13] As of 1938. See Homer Hoyt and L. Durward Badgley, *The Housing Demand of Workers in Manhattan* (Report to the Federal Housing Administration, 1939), p. 143.

[14] This figure results from the subtraction of the computed value of residential land from the total assessed value for all land.

[15] These data are substantially the same as those derived from application of the percentages of land in different uses to the total area of New York City and Manhattan (*Progress Report, op. cit.,* p. 34).

Use	New York (Square Miles)	Manhattan (Square Miles)
Residential	185.75	13.90
Non-residential	31.63	5.08
Parks, cemeteries	31.01	3.16
Vacant land	61.71	0.06
Total	310.10	22.20

The population in New York increased from 1920 to 1930 by 131,-040 persons per annum.[16] Between 1930 and 1938 the estimated increase was 70,168 persons per annum.[17] How long a time at this rate of increase would be needed to occupy the 61.71 square miles of vacant land and thus enable building value to be realized upon it; and how long if the 1920–30 rate of increase could be restored—a rather unlikely contingency? Again all will depend on the density:

Density of Families per Acre	Years Required at an Annual Population Increase of 131,040	Years Required at an Annual Population Increase of 70,168[*]
12	14.3	25.25
50	58.9	105.80
100	117.8	211.60

[*] The actual annual population increase for 1930–40 was noted below (n. 17) as 44,981 persons. If that figure is used, the number of years required to absorb the vacant land in New York at 12, 50, and 100 families per acre will be 41.2, 171.8 and 343.5 respectively.

If then the increase of population in New York maintains its present rate and if it be housed at the density now proposed for a certain housing scheme, the majority of the owners of vacant land within the city must wait 100 years and many of them 200 years before they will

---

[16] U. S. Census.

[17] Estimate by the New York City Department of Health, cited by Hoyt and Badgley, op. cit., p. 166.

Since this was written the data from the 1940 Census show the actual increase for the decade just ended to have been only 44,981 persons per year.

realize any value from use of the site for building purposes. If these facts are even approximately true and if present views on prices and densities continue, the conclusion seems to follow that the majority of this land has no real value whatever today and is unlikely to have any for generations to come!

Meantime the owners, on the strength of a gamble with odds of 100 or 200 to 1 against their sites being selected, are holding up their land prices which compel those very high densities which in turn increase the odds against them! By reducing the density to 50 dwellings to the acre the odds would be halved; by reducing it to 12, they would approach the kind of odds which gamblers are willing to face on the race course. To say that if present methods continue such land is really worthless, is indeed an understatement; for it is saddled with considerable yearly liability for taxes. If the annual tax payment is also to continue at present levels it would be interesting to calculate the ultimate loss on those acres which are the last to be occupied by dwellings. I have no figures for New York as to the extent to which the so-called tax structure is dependent on values not yet realized. I hope the taxing authorities may be able to tell us what is the total assessment on the approximately 61 square miles of vacant land in the city.[18]

There are, however, some remarkable figures for Chicago, showing what vast sums of purely fictitious value have formed parts of the tax structure there. In 1915 the total assessment was in round figures $2,000,000,000; by 1926 it had risen to $5,000,000,000; by 1933 the total had fallen to $2,000,000,000.[19] The whole of the taxes imposed during the intervening years on the $3,000,000,000 of increased assessment, or any part of it, must now be recognized as having been

---

[18] In *Premature Subdivision and Its Consequences* (Albany: Division of State Planning, 1938) at p. 88 Philip Cornick gives the assessed value of vacant land in New York City as $622,178,628. The area represented in that figure is not given but, if present vacant area is assumed (61.71 square miles), its application to the assessed value yields a value of 56 cents per square foot. Obviously, this is high, if 79 cents per square foot is the average value over the gross area of New York [see p. 220] and would indicate the inclusion of considerable fictitious value.

[19] These are the "aggregate values of the 211 square miles of land in the 1933 corporate limits of Chicago" as given by Homer Hoyt, *One Hundred Years of Land Values in Chicago* (Chicago: University of Chicago Press, 1933), Table LXXX, p. 470.

assessed on a fictitious capital value which never did exist and quite likely never will. Taxes, like other charges, cannot be collected from that which has no existence. However much may be assessed on fictitious values, that part of the assessment which is paid—for the default is large—all comes from the actual realized values for present use, and in fact falls on the actual income value of the property, or on other income which the owner may choose to tap for the purpose. Such fictitious values, so far from strengthening the tax structure, steadily tend to undermine it.

The case of Manhattan presents an aggravated condition not only because there is no increase of population to justify hope for increase in land value, but also because since 1910 the population has been falling rapidly, until now nearly 30% of the numbers once living there have already deserted it for more attractive dwelling places. As regards residential use, therefore, Manhattan is faced, not like New York as a whole with the problem of using to the best advantage a limited increase of population, but with that of creating conditions so attractive that the decrease may be arrested, and possibly some small share of the future increase attracted there. True, there is little vacant land on the island; but a recent survey has revealed that there are over four square miles of decayed areas[20] which call for redevelopment for housing purposes. The conditions now attached to these areas on the master plan allow a density of about 77 families to the acre which, if applied to the whole area, would house at 3.74 persons per family a population of 734,700 people.

Figures such as those used for Chicago are not available to show how much, if at all, the area occupied by buildings for purposes other than housing on Manhattan is increasing and could reasonably be expected to take up some of the land vacated by the emigrating population. In view of the recent development of very high business buildings, there seems no reason to expect much spread of this area, particularly as some at least of the city's business may be expected to follow the migrated population.

In regard to the return to be expected from the development of land for residential purposes, only the average sum per family has so far

---

[20] This figure appears to agree approximately with the estimated total of the areas which have been demarcated by the New York Planning Commission as ripe for clearance, replanning, and rehousing.

been considered. What a family can and will afford in rent for the site of its dwelling must be limited by its income. Those living in dwellings renting at less than $20 per month will obviously be most strictly limited by their income, as there will be little margin in most cases above what is needed for absolute necessities. Those with higher incomes will be in a better position to consider what they get from their payment in ground rent, a consideration very prominent in people's minds when purchasing any other commodity. Although it is not claimed that families, on average, will pay for the site of their dwellings pro rata with the area of which they have the enjoyment, the contrary suggestion that, on average, they will pay the same rent per dwelling however small the area which they can use or enjoy is no more reasonable. That area is reduced very rapidly with increasing density, because the extra dwellings occupy a greater proportion of each acre of land and usually call for additional road space, which again reduces the total free ground that has to be divided among the increased number of families.

If two-story houses be taken to occupy 48 square yards of ground, and apartments 90 square yards; if, further, an allowance for roads and public access paths be made of 54 square yards per house and 66 for each ground floor flat, irrespective of the number of stories, the following table will give the amount of free land per family which is available for purposes of amenity and recreation:

No. to the Acre	No. of Stories	Free Land per Family (Square Yards)
Single-family houses		
12	2	300
20	2	140
Apartments		
40	4	82
60	5	50
120	10	25
120	6	14.33

From this comparison of what is obtained at different densities, the contention that the return on land can be assessed at a fixed sum per family, regardless of the density, is surely as absurd as it would be to expect that the same price per acre or square foot for any given land can be expected or realized whatever the density that may be fixed. Somewhere in between these two unreasonable extremes will lie the truth; this means that reduced density may be relied upon to yield a higher total of value to the owners of land generally, but a lower sum per square foot than the fortunate owners of a few plots might receive if all the available developments could by means of high density be concentrated on a small area. Consequently low density must mean for the city a higher total of land value, and a more stable tax basis, whereas high density reduces the total land value and greatly increases the degree of uncertainty as to tax revenues.

From the point of view of the whole body of land owners and of the city, the early realization of value over larger areas of land and the more rapid redemption of blighted areas, which a lower density would promote, would be an adequate compensation for a considerable reduction in price per square foot. From the point of view of the tenants or occupants, a reduction in price, relatively much less than the reduction in density, would suffice to give them a much better, larger, and more attractive site and setting for their dwellings at so small an extra cost as to be well worth while paying. Costs of development per acre fall rapidly with reduced density; often considerably more rapidly than the reduction would indicate, whereas, as we have seen, the area available per family increases also in a ratio much more rapid than the rate of reduction. From the occupant's point of view, there is consequently a very rapid increase in the value of what he gets for his rent with reducing density, and this makes a somewhat higher payment per family well worth while. From the owner's point of view the increased area on which value is realized, a modest increase in the amount received per family, and in the total receivable together with the relatively reduced costs of development, bring an advantage which is of special importance at a time when the total available increase in population is rapidly diminishing and, unless some change takes place, will at no very distant date come to an end.

Where one-family dwellings, whether single or row houses, are concerned, the increased cost of development per acre, with higher density, and the increased proportion of land obliterated by buildings and roadways, result in a very rapid diminution of the area of free land available per family. Where increased density is obtained by adding to the number of stories, that is, by piling more families above one another on the same ground, there is a seeming avoidance of part of the increased costs of development. This avoidance is, however, seeming rather than real, and largely consists in shifting the cost from those responsible for the development to the broad shoulders of the public. High density of occupancy throws greater demand on all streets and services, to an extent not easily measured or allocated, but very substantial.

One aspect of the matter, however, can be quantitatively stated. A certain space per 1,000 persons is regarded as necessary for recreation in urban areas. The smallest standard generally regarded as satisfactory calls for 7 acres of space per 1,000 persons, that is, 33.88 square yards per person, or 127 yards per family of the size of 3.74 persons here taken. The table already given [p. 225] shows that with 12 houses to the acre, 300 yards per family are available; so that the 7 acres per 1,000 for recreation ground could be taken and yet leave 173 yards available for private enjoyment by each family. In the higher densities, however, no such provision could be made, and additional land must be found from some source for recreation space. In the case of the density of 100 families to the acre proposed for certain housing schemes, to comply with the standard, 12,700 square yards or 2.62 acres must be provided for every acre used for building. If this land is to be reasonably accessible, it will have to be bought in the neighborhood, at prices based largely on the expectation that 100 families to the acre could be housed on it. For every acre thus built upon, therefore, there should be added to the cost the price of another 2.62 acres to be acquired for recreation space. Where high densities are permitted, this cost usually falls on the public, through its parks department.

In this country, there is more experience in urban conditions of high density than of low, especially for the low-income groups. In England, on the other hand, there is ample experience of both high and low densities for such dwellings. The whole municipal housing scheme there affords a notable example. Of the 1,150,000 dwellings built by local authorities since 1919, about 1,000,000 have been built at an average density of 12 to the acre. The larger land owners were able to appreciate the value of realizing increment on a larger area, and often accepted a lower price per acre in view of the restriction. I should estimate the average price paid at about £275 per acre. The agricultural value of the land might average £50 per acre, leaving an increment of £225. Supposing double the density had been adopted, a somewhat higher price would certainly have been asked in some cases; but over the whole there would have been no great change, in view of the compulsory purchase powers possessed by the local authorities. Assuming the same price, the owners would have lost half their increment; the tenants would have lost two-thirds of their gardens or recreation space; and, because of the higher cost of development at double density, they would probably not have saved more than 10 or 12 cents per month in rent—a saving which would have been dearly bought by the loss of the garden or recreation land. Moreover, if the 100% increase in density had been accompanied by a 42% increase in land price, the tenants would have had to pay the same rent for the smaller area while the owners would still have received a greatly reduced total of land value.

From the above considerations and facts, there would seem to be urgent reason for the citizens of New York and of other American cities, as well as for the owners of land, to consider whether they would not all be far better off if they adopted a greatly reduced density of development accompanied by a reduced price per square foot of land, which, realized on a much larger area, would yield a greater total of value to owners, and would redeem blighted areas, not only at a greater speed, but in a manner which, because of the additional amenities and greater opportunities for recreation, would be much more likely to arrest the drift of population from the areas and secure their permanent occupation.

Index